My Sub-Lyme Life

Janet F. Murray

Parson's Porch Books

My Sub-Lyme Life
ISBN: Softcover 978-1-955581-71-4
Copyright © 2022 by Janet F. Murray

Parson's Porch Books is an imprint of Parson's Porch *&* Company (PP*&*C) in Cleveland, Tennessee. PP*&*C is an innovative organization which raises money by publishing books of noted authors, representing all genres. Its face and voice is **David Russell Tullock** (dtullock@parsonsporch.com).

Parson's Porch *&* Company *turns books into bread & milk* by sharing its profits with the poor.

www.parsonsporch.com

My Sub-Lyme Life

This book is a memoir about certain aspects of my life. My words reflect my present recollections of incidents over time. I have deliberately changed some names to protect the privacy of those involved. There is no intent to harm any of the characters mentioned in this work.

Contents

Dedicated to our parents –

Ray and Mary Murray

\

Introduction

No Regrets

That heading is not entirely true. I do have some regrets, such as not learning Latin American dances or traveling more. I have a curious nature and once enjoyed visiting new countries and meeting people of different cultures. Also, I regret not having had a normal relationship with my mother. Other than that, I don't spend time in sad contemplation, maybe because I have been accused of being highly practical, which leaves room for only occasional bouts of sentiment. When one is focused on survival, as I have been for many years, saving energy with every physical movement is the goal for the day - there is little energy left for much else.

Why? Quite simply – rickettsia infections. Rickettsia, burgdorferi on one side of the ocean; Lyme disease on another side. By whatever name, these miniscule, infinitely small spirochetes, or bacteria in more common parlance, carried by ticks, fleas, and other creatures, are exponentially destructive. They rob health and create enormous fear and confusion, especially when they escape the radar of a precise diagnosis. As a result, I stopped dreaming at age 17 as I had no idea if I would make it to my 21st birthday.

Now, decades later, apparently, I needn't have been concerned. Hindsight is 20/20, as everyone knows, and I have managed to remain employed and, until recently, to take care of myself. Sometimes, I think that I am similar to disabled animals who have little carts to support their useless legs so that they can carry on with their lives, not really knowing or thinking of themselves as being disabled. There is too much to be done, too much living to do or, more accurately in my case, sheer survival that drives my daily activities.

I cannot help but wonder how such tiny bacteria can do so much harm. I remain stunned that they are so incredibly ancient, sinister, and powerful. One small tick bite with a certain volume of bacteria injected into my body managed to all but annihilate a certain section of my nervous system that controls physical movement. Those few bacteria needed only a short time to produce nasty symptoms like full-body rashes, pins and needles, headaches, hair loss, anemia, poor sleep and brain fog, liver toxicity and, most inconveniently, a loss of the use of the vast majority of muscles in my body. Simple, effective, destructive, and deadly.

My hands still work well enough to type. So, every day, I sit at my desk, shoulders bowed. My head is heavy, weighing me down as I attempt to remain upright enough to continue typing away at the freelance projects that pay the bills. Difficult but still doable. I can move my legs outwards and inwards when sitting. Even if working for myself has not been easy, I count myself as lucky to be in this position, which brings me to another regret - that I didn't leave the corporate environment sooner to find online work.

Perhaps part of my will to battle on has been prompted by flashes that my mind and soul were somehow separate from my body. I felt that way long before any parasitic bacterial infections decided to squat within the realms of my flesh. This disconnect has been with me for as long as I can remember: my soul, mind, spirit have never felt integrated.

Despite my occasional fantasies about overcoming Lyme, I have become resigned to the idea that I will never recover my physical strength or experience the joy of corporeal movement again. I do ask myself: where did it all go wrong? How did this all begin? A long, long time ago. Not as far back as the prehistoric bacteria that invaded my life, but at least half a century.

Chapter 1

The Beginning

To reach, I lift my right arm with my left hand. In fact, to do most anything, I have to make the same maneuver. My right arm is the only appendage that works other than a weak ability in my fingers. Getting into bed or going to the toilet, I need to lock my elbows and use leverage and miniscule hip movements to inch myself into position. I wasn't always this way. Before being raped, before my first husband learned never to play with guns, before Lyme disease rudely invaded my body, my life had largely been sublime.

I was born in Keiskammahoek, a small, colonial South African village nestled between mountains with a river running along one border. About an hour's drive away from the nearest town, this quaint community featured large, gracious homes with the occasional government home (housing funded by the government for poor folks like me and my family) in between, a tennis club and a badminton venue for adults, several churches, and a junior and secondary school. The main street hosted most of the businesses. When I was about five years old, I remember buying sweets from a candy shop. After the purchase I wandered behind the building for some reason and was disgusted with the smell of raw cow hides hung in the sun to dry. The stench was unbearable in the heat of the day. It reminded me of the liver my mother forced me to eat and which I promptly regurgitated, unable to stomach the taste and texture of the offal. Our parents abhorred wasting food. Eating what our mother prepared was obligatory, especially if we wanted the taste of candy in our mouths following a meal.

An old-style colonial hotel provided a meeting point for locals and an overnight place to sleep for travelers on their way to somewhere else. Few people intentionally headed for a tiny, isolated community like Keiskammahoek. I recall the snooker table, elegant dining-room with several sets of cutleries for different courses, fancy glasses for alcohol, dark passageways leading to guest bedrooms, a vast array of knickknacks on the walls and a beautiful garden, as well as an old carriage *sans* horses, which was on display outside the hotel.

My parents often visited friends at either the "men only" bar or in an elegant lounge which was set aside for the ladies to listen to music on an old gramophone and keep a semi-watchful eye on the kids. The ladies' lounge was filled with old style photographs, paintings of old men, pipes and dogs and ornaments, all of which just spoke of forgotten times, which of course, few appreciated.

Overall, the community was a paradise that held great allure for myself and my four older brothers, Keith, Trevor, Ronald, and Robert.

I specifically recall Christmas functions where Mom dressed in a long evening gown with matching shoes and clutch bag and sang her heart out as she performed "Sweet Molly Malone" at the hotel event. My mother had an excellent soprano voice, but her talent was unfortunately confined to entertaining at functions held by the local hotel and in the Anglican church. The unrealized dream of a young women to become a recognized soprano singer took backstage for lack of opportunity, was replaced by raising a family.

Dad worked for the Department of Bantu Affairs, and Mom held an administrative position at a local garage owner for a while when she wasn't taking care of her family. Our government home featured large rooms, high ceilings and a garden that stretched seemingly forever and swelled with fruit trees, vegetables, and flowers. We all got our tiny little patch to plant poppies or whatever other flower seeds Mom managed to get her hands on. At the back of our home was a vast expanse of land, which blossomed with the sweet-smelling aroma of chincherinchees in the winter. Their delicate, snowflake blooms were an absolute delight to behold.

A furrow ran behind our home and served a magical playground where we spent our time in childish pursuit of tadpoles, frogs and crabs, the kind of critters that turned country life into the paradise that occupied our time outside of school. After the rains, we loved to play in the mud puddles and examine the earthworms that had come to the surface to escape a watery grave. When my three older brothers came back home after spending time in their boarding school in Adelaide, they too enjoyed going out into the field beyond the furrow to look for spiders and scorpions to pit against one another as only boys can do. Cleaning up after her children was a fulltime job for mom as she monitored her growing offspring.

A farmer kept some cows in the enclosed field in front of our home, while a horse stable belonging to someone else was situated at the end of the dirt road leading down from our home to one of the side roads off the main street. Turn right and the road led to the school and, farther along, the cemetery. Turn left to reach the main road, two short blocks away. The stable at the end of our lane did not belong to us, and we were told never to go near the horses in their stable or the cows in the field directly opposite our home. We knew that we would probably get a good hiding with a sjambok, leather belt, tomato box plank or wooden coat hanger if we did. Psychologists today will not agree with this approach, but we didn't particularly feel that way. For us, it was an infrequent part of life.

My mother baked the most amazing cookies, allowing us to lick the dish or eat bits of the raw, sweetened dough. Cookie baking days were wonderful as Mom made sure her sons were well stocked before their return to boarding school. She also filled our home pantry with canned fruits from the garden, including quince preserves and jams, along with our favorite biscuits. The only thing she made that I didn't like was liver or any other kind of offal, which still turns my stomach.

Family outings were largely limited to the badminton hall, which also served as a venue for visiting celebrities. For some reason, I was too shy to go up on stage when a touring magician called for volunteers to join him. No matter how much my mother tried to persuade me to join the others, my feet would not budge. I was paralyzed, too shy to make a spectacle of myself, and no amount of persuasion could get me to make that move. My nature was largely outgoing but when it came to being the center of attention on stage, as myself, I baulked. This diffident side followed me into my senior school years where acting was an absolute pleasure but speaking as myself in front of others or singing remained a terrifying prospect. As much as I was an extrovert growing up, I have remained an inherently private person throughout my adult years. Until now, of course.

Since my older brothers were at boarding school, I was left with Robert, who is about five years older than me. Waiting for my brothers to come home from boarding school or traveling through to the big cities of King William's Town or East London was another adventure of my young life. I remember being bitterly disappointed on a trip to King William's Town where we didn't get to see a Tarzan movie and when we took the long two to three-hour drive to East London to buy clothing for the older boys and not going to see the seals as my mother had promised.

Few incidents invaded our Eden. I seemed to suffer from regular bouts of tonsillitis during the first few years of my life. Other incidents involved fairly vociferous nosebleeds in the heat of summer while playing on the front lawn beneath a huge loquat tree. Other than that, my health was excellent growing up. I had no idea of what was to come and had no way of preparing myself for the shattered dreams to follow in other areas of my life at that innocent age.

Keiskammahoek back in the late 1960s and early 1970s was the perfect place to raise children. Every November, the town celebrated Guy Fawkes day by lighting a large bonfire in the field across from the tennis club and next to the doctor's office. Overall, my childhood consisted of having our own little garden patch to plant flowers, playing in the field and furrow behind our home, collecting wild creatures and having domestic pets ranging from dogs and cats to chickens and bunny rabbits, baking cookies for my brothers to give them comfort while at boarding school and many other outdoor pastimes. I fondly recall trips into the mountains over a weekend in an old Land Rover, traveling on narrow dirt roads with a sheer cliff on one side and mountain on the other just to reach the source of the ice-cold flowing river, drink its water, swim, bask in the sun and have a picnic. This all changed drastically when my father passed away, the first of many times when my life would lurch in an unknown direction, characterized by painful learning curves.

I never went back to Keiskammahoek. In the harsh light of reality, some things need to remain semi-pristine illusions.

Besides, later trips to our family home by two of our brothers and their wives illustrated the vivid decline of neglect that transformed a once beautiful, thriving country village into a drab, unproductive, dead space. My childhood paradise was no more, unknowingly, and seemingly paralleling my personal journey to some degree after our departure!

Chapter 2

Paradise Disrupted

The day Dad died, I don't recall what I was doing but remember Robert and I were at home. The older boys were at boarding school, but I have memories of hearing my mom's voice on the back veranda shouting to us to call the doctor. A brief attempt to use the phone proved fruitless since neither I nor Robert had ever used it before - there had been no need. No one had really shown us how it worked. Either that, or the switchboard operator was taking a break. In those days, all calls were channeled through the operator, allowing people to snoop on each other's conversations when the temptation arose.

Robert and I had no interest in snooping villagers at the time, not that either of us were aware of this portal of gossip. We had other things on our minds as our young brains desperately scrambled for ways to help our father. We decided to run to the doctor's office to get help. It was only a few blocks away from where we lived but we were small. I was only about five and Robert was nearly 10. I think Dad must have died on a weekend as we were met with closed doors when we arrived at the doctor's office. Having no luck there, we ran to the doctor's private home, several more blocks away from where we lived. There, we were confronted with quite a vicious looking Alsatian whose barks scared us. Tired, fearful, and defeated, we decided to run back home.

By that time, our mother had managed to get to the phone but was too late. Our father was about age 46. My last image of them together was Mom holding Dad in her arms while his heart gave out. Mom was about 39. Arrangements were made for neighbors to collect my two older brothers from boarding school in Adelaide. I don't remember whether Keith was serving time in the army at that point. What I do recall is that Robert and I landed up at someone's home with Mom. An older woman looked down at me, asked me if

I wanted a Disprin and said to no one in particular, "Don't worry. She is too young to understand what has happened," or words to that effect. Unfortunately, I did know what had happened. I knew our father was gone and was never coming back, and I'm pretty certain that Robert was fully aware of this fact as well. No Disprin was going to help or change that fact.

I was deemed too young to go to our father's funeral church service, but I remember where his grave is. Mom must have taken me with her when she went to visit the site, possibly before we left Keiskammahoek behind for the last time. I learned quickly that survivors move on, carrying on with life no matter what. That's a lesson that would stand me in good stead through the trials that lay ahead.

Looking back, I cannot imagine how difficult it must have been for Mom. Our relationship slowly deteriorated, too. She developed a constant need to control me, leading to repeated unconscious criticism, which dented my spirit more than any bacteria could have done. Now, much later, I understand just how much she had sacrificed for her family. Our mother was a tough lady, a hardy and an unrelenting survivor, with few filters, among her other qualities. Now in my 50s, I have only truly begun to see her for who she was. Despite everything, I am finally grateful that she raised me to be equally tough. Without this one quality of learning how to persist against the odds stacked against me, I might have surrendered a long time ago. My mother raised a survivor, a trait that would unwittingly serve me well in time to come.

Of course, from the perspective of a child in need of a mother's nurturing, her desire for bluntness and lack of a gentle filter - as Keith's wife Andi would in later years succinctly describe - won out and would lead to acrimony on my part and many who knew but failed to understand her. Mom's unbridled comments became a source of pain and strife in her relationships, leading to major misunderstandings, frustration, pain, and not a little heartbreak. Andi was probably one of the few people who understood Mom, empathized with her suffering, and probably proved to be a significant support for a woman whose loneliness and inability to connect on an emotional level with others, had caused her to withdraw even more from life.

The family dynamic had been set at a young age. My brothers and I found it difficult to understand or cope with the woman that our mother had become. Our love for her remained at a distance from an authoritarian figure who brooked little disobedience and had little emotional strength to deal with any further stress. The prickly dynamics of the parent-child relationships took a steep toll, and our tolerance levels were worn down by the brutal honesty that was our mother's preferred mode of communication.

I only really began to understand my mother while battling to survive my chance meeting with Lyme disease. We were both akin to a streetwise misfit whose own life had been so traumatized that she lost all knowledge of herself while straining to endure one more day. Sadly, by the time my eyes had opened to the person my mother was, dementia had her in a shockingly rapid vicelike grip. Our potential to communicate was all but gone.

After our father's death, my mom found a job as a hostel matron in Frankfort, another small village about two hour's drive away from Keiskammahoek. The car was packed with Mom, Robert and me, and our cat and dog menagerie of Stripes, Tiny, and Puppet. We took the long drive from Keiskammahoek to Frankfort to begin the next chapter. I have no idea what happened with all of the chickens and bunny rabbits, but I guess that was part of our lives that Mom had to leave behind. Keith quickly returned to military duty, which was compulsory then. My other old brothers went back to school in Adelaide. Slowly, life soon resumed a certain level of normalcy. That lasted about as long as I needed to leave Keiskammahoek behind.

Chapter 3

From Frankfort to Queenstown

We settled in the small community of Frankfort, which had been created by a legion of British and German settlers during 1857 and was the misspelling of the original Frankfurt in Germany. The Eastern Cape province of South Africa once welcomed a plethora of German and British settlers although little of the German culture and language seeped into the 20th century. We stayed there for about a year.

Mom, Robert, and I moved into the local hostel, which housed a small group of children from the local farming community since it was too far to drive them to school on a daily basis. The girls' and boys' dormitories were in separate buildings, and the school only provided tuition through standard five (grade seven nowadays). Mom occupied a flat down a long passageway quite far from where I shared a room with another girl. The older girls were housed in a large area adjacent but separate to my room on the way to Mom's flat. Our cocker spaniels mainly stayed with her, and I saw little of them from then on. Unfortunately, the journey had been unkind to Stripes, our cat, who apparently disappeared into the veld behind the hostel soon after we arrived in Frankfort. Decades later, Ronald told me that that Stripes had died. Mom had obviously tried to spare my feelings about losing a favorite member of the family.

So, began our new bittersweet adventure. I loved school in the beginning. We had the usual school activities such as tennis-set for the small kids. I still remember the white shirts, skirts and shoes with their basic orange soles and canvas tops that needed some kind of white liquid polish to keep them sparkling. No fancy track shoes for us like those developed in more recent years. We also had athletic days where each class held competitions in running, high jump, long jump, and relay races. The heat didn't bother us much because parents provided the snacks and cool drinks. I even took an adventurous ride on a big person's bicycle down the main dusty road running through the village.

Robert and I saw little of each other in this new environment. With the age gap between us, this was to be expected. Nevertheless, we still spent time together. While at the hostel, Robert contracted measles and was confined to a darkened sickbay where Mom continued to take care of him. Once he healed, I followed with my own bout of measles and recall how Mom had tried to get hold of one of the doctors in nearby King William's Town to check on me due to a high temperature. He refused. I survived anyway, the first of many times when I was better off staying away from the medical profession.

Not that long afterwards, the same doctor would diagnose a rash as an allergic reaction to nylon school clothing, an incorrect decision that cemented the downward trajectory of my health from that point on.

In between school and extramural activities, Trevor and Ronald were collected to spend school holidays with us in Frankfort and followed up on some of their favorite hobbies of capturing injured or rejected wildlife. Once, they brought an eagle owl with them from Adelaide, where they were allowed to keep wild pets as part of their greater education. The wee eagle owl then managed to escape, obviously having found its wings.

I was always a curious child growing up and quite driven when I had a goal or became fascinated with a project. Mom found me sitting up in bed one night after midnight, furiously knitting to complete the toy teddy bear project needed for a class. I was determined to get part or all of it finished before going to sleep and have little doubt that I accomplished what I had set my mind to.

In Frankfort, I remember that one older girl suggested we play glassy-glassy, a board game where a glass is used to supposedly summon demons or some kind of spirit. They created an impromptu Ouija board, found a glass, and the game began with questions being asked. I was pretty sure the older girls were deliberately moving that glass around the board. Still, that night was the second time in my life that I experienced a sense of fear. The first had been when I spotted a leguaan (a large monitor lizard) on our veranda back in Keiskammahoek. I was only 6 when I played glassy-glassy. I would have plenty more scares in the future. I would also return to the spiritual often in later years, and it remains a motif in my life. I just don't need a board anymore.

My lone year in Frankfort was a bit of a blur, but I remember something else that happened there. After settling into bed for the night, I was awoken by the sound of footsteps walking down the passageway outside my bedroom. They halted abruptly at the old telephone booth at the end of the passageway that had been installed to allow kids away from home to contact their parents when the sense of homesickness became too much. For the first time, I was afraid of sleeping with my head under an open window. In those days, burglar bars weren't necessary. Today, sleeping so close to an open window in the current political climate in South Africa is just asking for trouble.

Another incident occurred after my mother moved me into the big girls' dorm. The windows were much higher as the outside lane sloped down to some old toilets below. One night, I again heard footsteps walking down to the toilet outside when there should not have been anyone around. Spooky!

Mom, Robert, and I saw out the year in Frankfort with intermittent school visits from Trevor and Ronald, but it was time to move on again. Mom had found a more lucrative position as a hostel matron for a senior girl's school in Queenstown. There, however, we couldn't stay with Mom. Robert went to the boys' hostel for Queen's College while I landed in the junior girls' Jubilee hostel. I don't remember the name of the school I attended but recall that Queenstown was the biggest town I had lived in up to that point.

Our school had a couple of massive swimming pools and a huge gymnasium. I loved sports like swimming and was extremely active. I began playing netball and tennis and seldom saw Robert or Mom except over the odd weekend. I embraced life at the hostel and was invited to spend some weekends on family farms or at a newfound friend's home in the town. Like my peers, my life was meant to run the Cinderella course of leaving school, getting married and starting a family. Unfortunately, that reverie didn't include a Fairy Godmother. I could have used one, but apparently, they were in short supply.

Robert and I eventually ended up at two separate schools in King Williams Town. I lived with Mom in her quarters at the hostel. Robert must have also stayed there or was in one of the boy's rooms. In those days, we all walked to school as it was still safe to do so, and my junior school was only one or two blocks away. I started my new school career at Kaffrarian Junior School for Girls while Robert went to Dale College. I was then 8 years old and would remain at the same school until I matriculated in 1983, about 10 years later.

Chapter 4

King William's Town

I started at my new school in standard 2. Our class was still writing with pencils while waiting for teacher approval to begin using real ink pens. From a class of about 30 students, much to my chagrin, I was one of the last to be allowed to use a pen for schoolwork. My writing wasn't neat enough and didn't come close to comparing to the beautiful penmanship of my classmates. Ironically, I am a writer now probably because computers do not demand any kind of penmanship. Also, my physical capabilities no longer stretch to being able to write with a pen. Despite my problems with calligraphy, my school life was good. I fit in and made many friends while familiarizing myself with new surroundings.

Just as Queenstown had been a step closer to a larger town, King William's Town was much larger than Queenstown. The junior school was in sight of the senior school but there was little mixing. There were tennis courts adjacent to the school building, a concrete base and open wall to play ball against during period breaks, a huge swimming pool, hockey field and netball courts next to the girls' hostel and squash courts near the boys' hostel where Mom worked. I was still at the tennis stage but also enjoyed the swimming pool during physical training or gym classes in the summer months. We had art classes with a teacher I adored and, although I wanted to take ballet classes, Mom insisted I take piano lessons instead. Money was tight for a single parent with two kids still at school. Trevor may have started working by that time or was in his last year of school prior to commencing compulsory military training, and Ronald was probably also nearing the end of his schooling in Adelaide.

I kept falling asleep in class. The teacher spoke to Mom, who hauled me off to the doctor who prescribed some energy booster to keep suspected anemia at bay and me awake during instruction.

23

That worked even though this interaction with the medical profession was based on treating the symptoms and not the cause. I saw the same family doctor who had declined to come out to Frankfort to assist Mom with my dangerously high temperature when I had measles. The booster prescribed by this doctor helped me to regain my energy, and my junior school years became filled with the typical outings into the bush, acting in plays, playing with friends and homework.

One day, I hiked to Chief Sandile's cave to see where he took refuge during the 9th frontier war in 1873 in an attempt to evade capture by the British. Sandile, a Xhosa ethnic group hero, is recorded to have moved from the caves in the Pirie forest to the Bawa forest some 8 km away before being killed in a shootout with Fingo soldiers.

In standard two, I also developed a full body rash. Even though I had spent a lot of time outdoors with school trips into the bush and participated in Girl Scout hikes in the country, the doctor decided I had an allergy as noted earlier. He prescribed cortisone, then considered as a panacea for most everything. My mother was told to collect this from the pharmacy and apply it to my entire body. The rash showed up just before an Easter weekend. My mom invited a friend over for dinner, and I recall lying in bed the entire time, exhausted and itching like crazy. Nevertheless, the topical cream vanquished the rash, and I resumed normal activities. I couldn't stop wearing nylon since our school socks and underwear were obligatory, but this activity never again initiated a rash.

Around standard five, I joined my family on a journey to the huge city of Pretoria where Keith and Andi got married and held their reception under a massive marquee tent alongside a lake. Around that time, I was voted as head of one of our schoolhouses, of which there were four and which were simply groups to encourage inclusion. I also auditioned for a school play, which involved singing on stage. I enjoyed acting but having to sing in front of a crowd just made me croak. That was one of my more embarrassing moments. Worse, I had not inherited Mom's soprano voice. I was aware but hoped that when I opened my mouth and actually sang in public, my brain would transform my vocal cords. Another illusion shattered.

By this time, Mom bought a small house for the three of us. Robert and I had grown apart, not that we had ever been close due to our age gap but now we seemed to be even more distant even though living in the same house. He wanted nothing to do with his younger sister and, with a 12-year difference between Keith and myself, I might almost have been an only child at times. I continued with piano lessons and was able to transfer a lot of emotion into my playing, but I preferred the outdoors. I did not notice the slow, inevitable deterioration in my health that was almost imperceptible from month to month but abundantly clear from year to year.

In the interim, in standard five (grade seven), I participated in a town production of *Camelot*, produced, and directed by my drama teacher, and in a few other school and local town plays that were presented in the small-town hall. It was during the run of the *Camelot* play that Ronald came to collect me after my performance one evening and took me to the hospital. There had been a car accident involving family members.

He was on a break from the Army due to a head injury sustained when one of the vehicles he was in swerved to miss a donkey and overturned. He suffered a concussion, spent a few days in hospital and was then sent home. While recuperating, he took Mom and Robert to the local hospital to donate blood. While Ronald was driving back, attempting to ease into the main road from the hospital, he stalled the car. The drunk driver collided with it, injuring all three family members.

Mom ended up with a few cracked ribs and a broken collarbone but was stable. Robert's injuries were far more serious. He had sustained a brain injury and was transported to the East London hospital where he lay in a coma for approximately three weeks. The driver had worked for a petrol station in town, arrived at work intoxicated and been fired. He had apparently then taken the work vehicle and had picked up speed when he saw the stalled vehicle in front of him and fled the scene after the collision. Attempts afterwards to track him down met with repeated failure, although I do not know how much effort was put into catching him.

The Road Accident Fund (RAF) donated a collection of encyclopedias to the family for Robert to continue his education once he returned home since he had just missed completing his last school year. That was not exactly helpful.

We went to visit Robert in East London over weekends. There was a lot of confusion, fear, and doubt about the future. No one could predict if or when he would come out of his coma, but one certainty was that when he did, it would be a long road to recovery. In time, Robert did return home and had to learn how to walk, eat and speak again. Whatever medication he was on seemed to exacerbate mood swings. Eventually, Mom found a place in Queenstown where he could get help. He was not fond of the rehab center and moved to Durban, before landing in jail due to possession of marijuana. Fortunately, Mom had support through church members, some of whom were also attorneys and who used their contacts in Durban to get Robert released.

Looking back, I can see how his physical injuries seemed to serve as a mirror for mine, because our mode of walking shared many similarities. However, while Robert had sustained injuries from a drunk driver using a car as a weapon, I had been hit by something much smaller.

Chapter 5

Senior School

My senior school years were quite dull and boring, but I still enjoyed the hiking weekends, drama classes and other activities. I also participated in exciting functions where the guys and girls got to mix at parties or through debating competitions and house plays.

My daily exercise consisted of walking some 10 km a day to school and back home and then to some sporting activity and back home. On route, I began to notice that the heel of my right foot kept catching the ankle of my left foot. At the same time, walking around the large school buildings between classes and up and down the stairs was also becoming taxing. I couldn't understand why but was aware that muscle weakness had begun several years earlier when I hiked to Sandile's cave and battled to climb up the steep mountain paths while my peers overtook me. Considering all the sports I played, I should have been close to super fit and, yet was struggling to keep up with schoolmates who were far less athletic.

Having befriended Frances, a classmate who lived at the hostel, I spent a few holidays with her. During one of these breaks, Frances and I had walked off the main road to jump down onto the riverbank to take a short cut. As I jumped down, my legs gave out under me. I landed on the sand with my legs folded under me. I had also noticed that I struggled to get up from a seated position on the ground during lunch breaks at school, where my friends managed this action with ease.

Frances came into my life with an extra bonus. She had an older brother Will who had a friend Anthony: tanned, blonde, and good looking. I fell in love with Anthony when I was in about standard seven or eight. We went out for a few years while I was in high school while he landed in the navy. Frances and I, Anthony, Will, and a bunch of their friends enjoyed parties in Port Alfred, lazy days on the beach, Christmas and New Year's eve celebrations. At one of these parties, I lit one of Anthony's cigarettes and became hooked. I have smoked ever since. We had a lot of fun together, interspersed with breakups and make-ups, doing the typical teenage things, which included alcohol. During the late 1970s and early 1980s, we had no need of other drugs. Later, kids from bigger cities who were a lot wiser than small-town teenagers like me introduced drugs. There probably was some marijuana smoking going on in town and worse, but I wasn't aware of this.

As with many schoolgirl romances, my relationship with Anthony also came to an end. Anthony coldly told me that he was breaking up with me because I had put on too much weight. This breakup must have occurred during my last year of school as I had added weight despite all of my physical activities. By then, weight loss pills had become the norm for me - when I could afford them. With every crash diet, I quickly managed to accumulate more weight. As a result, I climbed from a size 10 to a size 14 while in senior school, frequently hovering around a size 12. A few years later, Anthony knocked on my window in the early hours of the morning to tell me how much he missed me and that he wanted to get back together. I had lost some weight by then, but the hurt remained. I refused his advances.

Trevor married Cheryl who was a single child from a family with a German heritage. We attended their wedding and reception in an old public hall in town. Mom and Cheryl did not get along, partially due to the fact that Mom not surprisingly butted heads with Cheryl's mother. This situation caused the kind of disharmony that lingered far longer than the smell of a liver dinner. My three older brothers soon were married and parents. Trevor and Cheryl had a pair of children, Kyle, and Stacey. Ronald married Felicity and had two children, Craig, and Lisa. Keith and Andi found a home in Durban and had produced three boys, all with a different hair color at birth: Sean the blonde, Bruce the brunette and Derrick the redhead - a throwback to Mom's red hair.

Around the time I graduated high school, Mom sold the house and moved into the Anglican church rectory to take up a caretaker/secretarial position. Concerned about my physical health and not knowing quite what was happening to my body, I used to run up and down the steep stairs in the high tower that formed part of the church in an effort to increase my fitness level. It had little effect, but the view from the top was amazing. I guess that was some level of compensation for my diligence back then.

Having noticed my changed walking gait, Mom took me to see a specialist at the local hospital during what was probably one of his weekly or monthly visits from East London. Mom no longer had a car, which had been totaled in the earlier accident, so we took a long walk up the steep inclines to reach the clinic at the back of the hospital. The specialist conducted a few tests, including smacking me on the knees with a metal hammer to check my reflexes. He then asked me what I wanted to do after I left school. I mentioned that I wanted to go into acting or modelling but the look on his face was enough to let me know that was never going to happen. I burst into tears with the sudden awareness that something was wrong with me and that I was unlikely to realize any of my dreams.

The specialist suggested I go to Groote Schuur Hospital in Cape Town for further tests. I got a lift to Cape Town, where I stayed with the parents of an old school friend who then took me to the hospital. There, I was booked into the neurology ward for female patients and idled for a couple of days before tests began. I had a muscle biopsy done by a doctor who complained about having to cut through fat on my thigh just above the knee to obtain a sliver of muscle. This was a second biopsy; the initial sliver having been cut from my left calf muscle by the first specialist I had seen in King William's Town. Results from the first test had been inconclusive, hence my referral to Groote Schuur. I was so humiliated by the doctor's remark about my being fat since I was still young, sensitive, and impressionable. His words dovetailed too nicely with Anthony's parting insult.

I also felt isolated and was upset even further when one of the male patients from the neurology ward interrupted my bath one evening as there were no locks on the doors. The humiliation didn't end there. One of the specialists wanted to present my case to several other doctors. I didn't feel there was anything unreasonable about his request until he asked if I was prepared to stand on top of the meeting room table to demonstrate my walking. I completely baulked at the idea. Get on a table like a performing monkey? In a hospital gown, which was open at the back? That wasn't going to happen. Why they could not observe my gait down a quiet passage was beyond my comprehension? I returned to my hospital bed - disappointment filling my throat like bile yet again.

The biopsy results came back, and these experts claimed that I had the beginning stages of sporadic distal myopathy, a catchall term for rare genetic disorders when the doctors can't make a definitive diagnosis. A genetic specialist came to discuss the illness with me and later learned I had no family history of such a disease. Besides, the diagnosis didn't feel right. My strong sense at the time was that the diagnosis had been based on guesswork. Family members, however, went for their own blood tests as there was obviously a concern of passing this down to their children. Their results were negative much to everyone's relief, but that still didn't solve my health issue. I recall that these tests involved checking CK (creatine-kinase) levels, which indicated the level of protein in the blood due to the breakdown of muscle tissue. There was no such history in our family although none of us could trace our genealogy too far back.

There was a good reason for that. Our family tree had roots none of us knew about until Mom decided after my futile hospital stay that I was mature enough to withstand another bombshell. She calmly told me how her mother had been drugged and raped by a Greek café owner. As a result, Bessie became pregnant and had given birth to Mom. This was in the early 1930s, and the shame must have been so great for the family that Mom was led to believe that her grandmother was her mother. According to Mom, she enjoyed the company of her "mother" and had been informed that

Bessie was her older sister. That changed when at age 12 Mom learned the truth, which must have been a rude awakening and completely wrecked her understanding of the world. It didn't do much for me either, since hearing that Mom was born as the result of a rape raised questions about familial diseases. We also had loose family ties on my father's side, so tracing our genealogy for health reasons was impossible.

I was no closer to solving what was wrong with me and would spend many years on a sustained search for answers.

A second trip to Tygerberg hospital followed a few years after my stay at Groote Schuur. There, I had some other tests done to check brain functionality in another vain effort to pinpoint the cause of my muscle weakness. By this time, the diagnosis had changed to some other form of muscular dystrophy. More guesswork. To add insult to injury, I was sent back to King William's Town with a prescription for prednisone, a corticosteroid that replaces substances which are usually produced by the body and are needed for normal functioning. I counted: there are more than 40 possible side effects. I developed several of them, including a moon face and extra hair. I had so much hair on my head that the hairdresser had to use double the product to perm or color my hair.

None of the doctors mentioned to my family doctor that he needed to stay in contact with the neurology specialists in Cape Town. As a result, I took prednisone for six unnecessary months with no change in my condition other than the extra hair and extremely painful knee joints. Due to muscle weakness, my knees became tremendously sore from all my walking to the point where morphine did little to relieve the pain.

I felt that I had been a guinea pig in doctors' experiments and was angry at their arrogance in guessing at my diagnosis rather than being honest enough to admit that they didn't have a clue.

Amid all this probing, I still had to earn a living. I started working part time at a local retail clothing store over weekends and promptly developed incredibly painful heels from standing for long hours. We weren't allowed to sit during our work shifts even when no customers were around. I tried walking to work in high heel shoes, but after several twisted ankles, I reverted to flats. Finding suitable flat shoes in the future would present another challenge as the presence of a heel one centimeter too high sabotaged my mobility. This elevation would result in having to find a cobbler to make alterations, an additional expense on an already stretched budget. These small hurdles were just a foretaste of what was still to come. With the tortoise-like progress of whatever disease ailed me, I became increasingly aware of what lay ahead.

While renting a room in a church rectory, I began a full-time job as an articled clerk for a legal firm in King William's Town. This job was my real introduction to the working world. Mom took me shopping for work clothes, but I had a major fling after graduation before beginning work in January 1984.

Chapter 6

The School Girl Becomes a Very Confused Working Girl

I took the job at the legal firm as the first step toward studying for a law degree. Articling was just a glorified administrative position. I was supposed to work under the supervision of a lawyer for a minimum of two years, and following completion of my degree, would qualify to take the bar exam. The position required basically doing whatever the lawyer didn't want to do. On occasion, I would leave the office to visit the magistrate's court and the supreme court in Bisho. I also got to drive the senior partner to a hearing at Fort Hare University where I took notes. I cannot remember what the case was about but do recall that the senior partner sent me back to collect his huge, heavy briefcase from the car. I believe this was a ploy to get rid of me for a while as he didn't have the patience to wait for me to laboriously climb several sets of stairs into the building while dragging myself up with the help of the railings.

Working for this legal company enabled me to meet a lot of people, make friends and gain work experience. Because I was sent out to collect customers from the Amatola hotel, I got to go to the casino in the Ciskei and was able to visit the small outlying towns such as Fort Beaufort, Alice, and others. I also managed to dent one of the firm's cars in the parking lot. Unfortunately, studying towards a law degree proved more difficult than the rosy pictures my mind conjured up. Besides, my thoughts were far more focused on leaving home, partying, and looking for love in all the wrong places. I was able to pass about three or four subjects before becoming stuck on the third Latin book (no longer a prerequisite for this degree in South Africa). My foray into the legal environment lasted about two years until I decided to switch to becoming a legal secretary, primarily because the income was much better, and Latin was not required.

With my new salary, I was finally earning enough to move out of the church rectory. Before I did that, Mom let me in on another family secret. The closet was really open now. She confided in me how she became pregnant out of wedlock (a huge scandal back in the 1950s) after an affair with a married man. Unable to care for the child - she was a young woman herself and possibly still training as a nurse or nurse's assistant in Port Elizabeth - she gave up her first child for adoption. Years later, once the age for revealing such adoption records had passed, her daughter, Miranda, would find Mom and build a relationship with her that lasted until Mom died in 2018, approximately 27 years after they met as adults. At one point, Mom persuaded me to take a trip to Port Elizabeth to meet Miranda at the airport for the first time. For whatever reason, we had little contact for a long time until I visited Madeira with my second husband. After that, she played a significant part in my life.

A friend, Marie-Louise, also rented a room at the rectory. The two of us got along so well that we decided to share an apartment with one of my work colleagues - Colleen. Being of a similar age, we were keen on going out and meeting young men, partying, and having a good time. We spent a lot of our free time at a small nightclub on the outskirts of King William's Town. We were young and intent on enjoying ourselves, with alcohol always being at the center of our activities.

Troubled followed. I double-dated once with Marie-Louise who had been going out with Nathan for a while. His uncle was coming to town for a visit, and I was to be his company for the evening. We went out to a restaurant, had some good food and wine, and then went back to Nathan's apartment. During the evening, Marie-Louise and Nathan disappeared to his bedroom. The uncle and I sat on the floor in another room, while he plied me with booze and insisted on having sex with him. I tried to resist and told him "No," but I had too much to drink. He didn't care anyway.

Afterwards, I called Marie-Louise. The look on my face was unmistakable. She knew immediately something was wrong. Nathan drove us home. Date rape. I did not call the police. I probably should have, but I was drunk. I could imagine how the questioning would have gone. I was probably around 18 years at the time.

Soon after, I met Lebrandt at the nightclub over a weekend when he had come to visit his parents. We hit it off immediately, and he was to become my first husband after dating for close to 10 years. Lebrandt was studying human relations at Port Elizabeth University, so it became my mission to find a lift down to see him over weekends. In a small town, someone always knew of someone else taking the 3-hour trip to Port Elizabeth for various reasons. The commuters were usually young and welcomed another person to help pay expenses. So, began my long-term relationship with a privileged Afrikaner who came from a farming family and had butlers to serve their meals. Since I came from a less-affluent background, our relationship was not well accepted by Lebrandt's family. I never felt comfortable in their company, specifically with his mother and sister. Among other things, they believed I had some genetic fault that I would pass onto our children - if we ever had any.

Back in the office, I was becoming bored with the trajectory of my career. I left the law firm and got a receptionist/secretarial position at a distillery that was operating in King William's Town. I stayed there for a year or so. In the interim, Lebrandt found a job at a government defense company in the Western Cape. Maintaining a relationship across 1000 km with only a landline for contact became difficult. I managed to procure one lift down to see him with a colleague who had arranged to travel to Cape Town for plastic surgery. While Lebrandt was at work, I drove his car to the beach to tan while waiting for him to get home. We spent a great long weekend together. After approximately one year in that position, Lebrandt found work in Cape Town.

Then 25, I realized that I wasn't going to die young. However, I was also aware that my physical mobility had been impacted and that a diagnosis of some form of muscular dystrophy would simply continue on a slow but inexorable trajectory towards life in a wheelchair. By then, I was embarrassed to walk outside because the strangeness of my gait had become more noticeable, and I needed a wall or other object to stabilize my movement. People must have thought I was tipsy. I became increasingly aware that I was attracting an audience while climbing stairs and negotiating the divide between the pavement onto the street or even the short steps into shops. I didn't help matters by falling flat on my face while pushing a shopping cart. Funny for onlookers perhaps but with that internal dread of where this was all going to end, I missed the humor. Even though I managed to fall in front of women from our church who were kindly concerned for my wellbeing, I wasn't comforted. By this time, my walking looked much like the way Robert walked as he recovered from the car accident. I wondered if my body was somehow mimicking his gait in some kind of unconscious empathy or whether I had some brain damage in an area that resulted in the similarity of our movements when walking.

Church revival/healing sessions were no less painful than some embarrassing moments navigating stairs with dozens of eyes watching my every move. I became outraged after being persuaded to go to one meeting with a healing session. Imagine attending a healing service in good faith only to be told in no uncertain terms that some imagined wrongdoing had led to a mysterious disease and that there was basically no hope. I left that service with even more guilt and shame on my shoulders, wondering what the hell I had done to deserve this and how on earth I could make it right.

One day, when I was around 25, I decided that guilt was just a waste of my time and energy. I wasn't such a terrible person that I should be faced with coping with a nameless disease. I might not have been the nicest person since I said and did as I pleased, but so did my group of friends. We were having what we thought to be innocent fun, weren't intentionally harming anyone, and were just trying to live our young lives. How could that anger the heavens?

Decades later, I would make friends with another lady who told me that her experience of God had been far warmer. Maybe it was because of the Anglican Church's teachings or the fact that Mom was quite a manipulative person and used emotional guilt to persuade me to her point of view, but the God I was raised with was not a particularly loving one.

Even a trip to a psychologist in East London in an attempt to find answers proved fruitless. Driving an old Mazda that Mom had bought for me and which I had to repay, I arrived for my appointment and spoke to the lady psychologist - Lillian. Although financially set, she had obviously not been practicing for a long time. I was made to sit on a bench in her office, which was in a big building alongside the main house, while Lillian plunked herself behind her desk about eight meters away. The situation was uncomfortable, and I struggled to open up to her in any meaningful way.

For my second appointment, I found her office empty and knocked on the front door of the private home. Big mistake. I was scolded and told that I had been instructed on my first appointment not to invade her privacy. I felt humiliated, and the rest of the session was a waste of time and money. My interactions with doctors, specialists and now this psychologist were fast persuading me as to the limited usefulness of the medical profession. Clearly, I was on my own. Equally clearly, I would never go back to that psychologist with her fabulous degree in her fabulous home along the river. The abortive talks ended that foray into resolving my confusion and desperation. By then, I felt there was absolutely no framework of safety and security.

Chapter 7

Gordons Bay

Lebrandt and I met when I was about 19. I was 25 when we moved into our new home in Gordon's Bay. Lebrandt's mother was not far behind. She continued to try decorating our home, well-intentioned no doubt but not entirely well received. My relationship with his older sister also continued to be a nonstarter with her spreading rumors about having been to a psychic who had told her falsely that I had been pregnant and aborted a child. Both sister and mother also were sure I had affairs while dating Lebrandt. I did see a couple other men, but not once the relationship with Lebrandt grew serious. His family didn't notice the distinction. As a result, our new beginning together was fraught with underlying tension and would have been even if I hadn't been seeing anyone else. My resentment towards his mother and sister obviously didn't help the situation.

I started my new job in Bellville. At first, I drove alone and then established a carpool, which later ended with myself, and another woman being driven to Bellville by a gentleman driver. It was an absolute relief to no longer have to drive 120 km a day although we spent more time on the road. During winter, we left home in the dark and returned at night. Rest was not an option. I kept busy sewing curtains for our home, preparing meals, doing the washing and so on. I enjoyed being a homemaker, but the stress eventually began to affect me despite my youth and energy.

I recall hanging up washing in the dark one evening, having to hold onto the washing line with one hand to maintain my balance while reaching down to grab an item of clothing with the other. I stepped into a small hole in the lawn and ripped the washing line, causing the clean laundry to land on the grass. I had to call Lebrandt to help and was amazed that he was angry with me for having wrecked the washing line. My walking and balance at that stage had deteriorated to the point where I was largely lurching from one handhold to the other. Where these supports weren't present, it was like walking the gangplank on a pirate ship.

Later, I insisted he begin ironing his own clothes since the work was just getting too much for me. Coming from a wealthy background and being accustomed to his mother doing everything, he was unprepared for such tasks. Unfortunately for him, I wasn't anything like his mother, which is possibly why he offered little support for me. I didn't help matters by being possessive and jealous. In time, I wondered if Lebrandt was so attentive to his parent's needs because, otherwise, he faced being dropped from their will. I have no idea, nor will I ever know, if my suspicions had any merit.

All of these tensions and stresses resulted in a trip to a doctor for anti-depressants. After two weeks, I discovered that I was supposed to have taken the medication in the mornings and not the evenings. Regardless, the medication didn't make me feel any better. I never took it again. My headaches had reached a point that I was taking up to eight codeine laden Syndol tablets a day for three to four days at a time with little relief. I didn't even get sleepy. The only way to really get through recurring cluster/migraine headaches was to sleep it off but that wasn't possible with a new job. For some reason, my boss frowned on my taking naps at my desk!

I continued searching for clues as to what was wrong with me and pursued some physiotherapy in Somerset West, homeopathy, water aerobics and the like. Because our finances were tight, I was not able to continue with many of these activities for very long. No matter how much exercising I did, my muscle strength did not improve. If anything, I continued to become weaker and weaker physically as the years passed. This physical deterioration and the peculiarity of my gait continued to attract unwanted attention when in shopping centers, with people staring at me without even acknowledging my presence. They were so focused on the strangeness of my movements that any sensitivity they might have had was simply lost in the moment. I found this incredibly humiliating but was at a loss as to what to do about it other than to avoid being in public as much as possible or learn to accept the invasive stares. At times, I would stare back, glare back or make a brusque comment, which seemed to shock some out of their rude reverie, but I realized I was fighting a losing battle.

Since the internet still hadn't made its way to South Africa, I registered with the local Strand library and indulged my interest in alternate worlds: metaphysics, the mysteries of the unknown and self-healing. I was a voracious reader and purchased as many of Deepak Chopra's books as possible. Louise Hay's wisdom also formed a part of my foray into the last frontier of the human spirit and its inextricable link to the physical body and emotions. I read the *Third Eye* by Lobsang Rampa and did as much research as I could in color and sound therapy while looking for more information regarding the electric body as part of the physical body. Anything that had to do with healing, or the unseen fascinated me and held me spellbound in the knowledge that there was a world beyond my senses and that emotions impacted health. I learned about psychics, clairvoyants, and empaths in my quest to find answers to what physical disease I had and how or whether this had been impacted by my internal emotional and mental world. I built on my knowledge and fascination with this magical world beyond our senses by reading Rhonda Byrne's *The Secret*, M. Scott Peck's *The Road Less Traveled*, James Redfield's *The Celestine Prophecy* and several of Edward Cayce's books among many others in this genre. Still, I did not stumble across the answers I sought.

What I did find was an advertisement in the newspaper about Christian Science and went to visit the man who had placed the advertisement. The book he gave me, entitled *Science and Health*, was apparently the mainstay of Christian Science, having been written by the founder of this movement, Mary Baker Eddy. I found it incredibly difficult to read and understand. It was quite technical, but the interpretation of Christian tenets made sense to me insofar as I was able to assimilate this knowledge.

Nevertheless, my avid reading introduced me to the world of the unseen, the world of energy, and I finally felt at home.

Although I struggled to grasp this concept in the beginning, the more I read, the more sense the idea of invisible energy made and the more I delved deeper into this world. Many of the books I collected contained guidelines regarding meditation, quiet mindfulness, conscious awareness and how our thoughts affect our emotions and just about everything else in life. I learned that we are all transmitters and receivers in an invisible, electric form. My reading also explained how a higher intelligence (or God) could be everywhere all the time and that this intelligence was in everything and waiting to be harnessed. This concept told me that we are all in control of our world if we choose to put in the effort to develop our spiritual worlds. Most of us simply take the easy way out by believing in a God and a devil, the latter of which who receives the blame for most things that go wrong. That perspective never seemed plausible to me. I felt I held the power within myself to heal, although the confidence and inner knowing had not yet pervaded my awareness.

As fascinating as this world of the invisible was, my attention was divided, and I never really spent the necessary time on meditation and affirmations. I had to focus on work and maintaining the household. Travelling long hours, getting up early and arriving home late was not particularly conducive to improving my spiritual world. Besides, the mental energy needed to enhance my wellbeing on various levels did not seem worth the effort. In truth, I did not quite believe the readings and doubted my own ability to harness the information and to translate it into practical results.

I had a great library, but my body was definitely not impressed.

During this time, I focused on the work of Christian Science and a particular set of affirmations contained in the book. *I Am.* The great spiritual I Am: "I am truth, I am light, I am life, I am love, I am spirit, I am soul, I am that I am." I needed another 20 years or so to assimilate an understanding of what Christian Science and *A Course in Miracles* meant by the phrase, "I am that I am," a momentary enlightenment on my journey to greater discoveries. At the time though, I did what I could in the couple hours a day available to me to experiment with these affirmations. I probably did this for about a month, and the affirmations filled my mind during whatever I did, including my regular swimming or other exercises.

After a few weeks, I got into my car on a Saturday morning and felt that I could lift my left leg up onto the clutch a lot more easily. This surprised me until my logical mind took over. Was I slightly stronger because I had been swimming regularly or were the affirmations actually working? Looking back on this situation several years later, I decided that I had strengthened my body through the use of these affirmations. I no longer had any doubt that they had been successful and that I had given up too soon. Life and doubt had supplanted self-healing. Mental efforts to duplicate this situation were half-hearted and doomed to fail. I had doubted myself and paid the price. One day, I hope to develop the discipline, interest, and energy to try this again. Visualization is the language of spirit, and generating positive vibrations is clearly the way to a healthier life on every level. This is the simple recipe but the practice and understanding or assimilation of this knowledge is a tad more complicated.

What I realized from my studies was that affirmations have two purposes. Firstly, they block unwanted negative thoughts; second, they imbue the mind and body with positivity for the brief periods they are practiced - unless you persist until they become habit. Many self-help books on the market have addressed the value of affirmations in making positive changes to lifestyle and health. They are seemingly simple to implement in theory, but the mental discipline required to apply this technique can be a stumbling block dependent on the depth of the desire to change in relation to ongoing daily challenges. That is not an excuse but simply a deduction that when you want something badly enough, you will go out of your way to make that happen. When you don't achieve your goal, it may simply not be the right time, or the person may not be ready or have other priorities that take preference ahead of the goal. One can look at this concept from so many different angles, but one thing is certain: goal achievement on any level is a very personal journey, a unique experience, and one that is not possible to learn vicariously since knowledge assimilation and understanding are different. I may understand an issue on a mental level. However, until this is comprehended at a heart or emotional level, it will remain dormant information.

Amid these studies, Lebrandt and I continued with our lives with the monotony of work and home chores being broken by visits with friends, various activities and the continued drama between myself and his parents. We never discussed their dislike of me. That would have been far too impolite for their genteel natures, but I sensed I would never be good enough in their eyes. Lebrandt and I ended up going on a couple of holidays with them and one or two other outings since we could not afford a holiday on our own. They were obviously good, decent people, but our personalities and experiences of life clashed. Where they were focused on routine and doing the "right" thing, my boundaries were not so well-defined.

I despised authority, and my mother-in-law was a former teacher, making her a dominant figure in our lives, not unlike that of my own mother with whom relations were also tenuous. I valued my freedom and being able to make my own decisions; they valued appearances. Lebrandt and I considered breaking up a few times in the four to five years we spent in the Western Cape but realized that neither of our incomes were sufficient to support our lifestyles on our own. So we decided to stick it out and became engaged. To maintain some level of peace, I tolerated his family. They attempted to do the same with me, knowing full well they had the upper hand. I continued to accept the lack of support from Lebrandt because I loved him.

Our engagement led to our marriage after Lebrandt's brother started a business in East London and suggested that Lebrandt resign from his job and move back. After having been in a relationship for close to 10 years, I was not willing to follow him without a concrete commitment. He agreed. All of these decisions took place in such a short space of time that I was left alone to resign my position, pack up the house and arrange our wedding in September in Somerset West, chosen because most of our friends were there. Lebrandt had already departed for East London and would return to the Western Cape for the ceremony. Then we would both leave to start our new life in East London.

My search for a wedding dress, shoes, venue and more began. I had a work contact who could arrange for discounted prices for VO5 10-year-old brandy and wine. I found a beautiful guesthouse and restaurant in Somerset West for our morning wedding. Finding someone in Cape Town to make lace up boots that supported my ankles was quite a mission, but I was successful. I sent out invitations, started packing up the house in readiness for the movers and continued with our wedding plans. I found a boutique that rented wedding dresses and planned the seating arrangements for our champagne breakfast wedding. There wasn't a chapel at the guesthouse/restaurant, but we were legally allowed to be married under a roof on the veranda, surrounded by witnesses, guests and a beautiful garden. Because I had total control over the wedding plans, I made sure that my dearest sister-in-law would not be sharing our table. Mom traveled from the Eastern Cape to give me away. None of my other family members were able to make it to my wedding due to finances and the distance, so I was glad that Mom could at least be there as I had met the majority of our friends through Lebrandt.

We were married on September 29, 1995. My new husband demonstrated his commitment by going back to his sister's house to watch a rugby match with a large number of the guests in the afternoon. Needless to say, I was less than impressed. After the game ended, we packed the car with what was left of our luggage and drove a couple of hours outside the Strand to spend our honeymoon evening at another guesthouse on the way back to the Eastern Cape. The next day, we drove 10 hours to East London and took up residence in a townhouse purchased by Lebrandt's brother and rented out to us. Our lounge suite was provided courtesy of Lebrandt's family as was our bed, both of which were family heirlooms. Lebrandt began work at the franchise, and I began unpacking boxes and making our new home comfortable.

Chapter 8

East London

Obviously, our first evening and weekend in East London had to be spent with Lebrandt's family. Lebrandt had taken over the management of a fast-food franchise. I spent time with him at the business in the evenings and got to enjoy the food, which was a treat as our finances did not allow for many meals at restaurants. This business was later sold as it was not particularly profitable, and Lebrandt was appointed to manage a small micro-loan business his brother had also started in Bisho. At times, I accompanied Lebrandt on the 80-minute drove to Bisho to help him in this business.

Lebrandt took the proceeds from the sale of our house in Gordon's Bay and invested it in his brother's microloan business with the intention that he receive 20 percent of the profits. He had to take care of the micro-loan business while waiting for the sale of the fast-food franchise to go through, placing him under enormous pressure. He had some relief over weekends, as the microloan business was closed then. He only needed to go into the fast-food outlet in the mornings and evenings to check that everything was on track. To cope, he transferred his affection to guns. He had also helped me to purchase a semi-automatic in Bellville before moving to the Eastern Cape. Together, we were able to go to a shooting range for some target practice. I became a pretty good shot, but guns were Lebrandt's interest and not mine.

Between September and December, busy with setting up in a new house and Lebrandt managing two businesses, most of our free time was spent at his parents' home: evening meals during the week - Saturday barbecues, Sunday lunches. My mother-in-law made sure that she was in control and was going to spend as much time with her son as humanly possible. Her tactics did not endear her to me although Lebrandt was clearly comfortable with being part of a close-knit family who enjoyed one another's company. This situation was foreign to me. My own siblings and I were so widely dispersed that spending time together was nearly impossible. For the most part, I didn't object although I didn't enjoy either situation.

By the time December rolled around, Lebrandt and I took out the staff of the franchise for a celebratory Christmas meal and looked forward to a short break between Christmas and New Year. He arrived home on the evening of the December 24, hauling computers that he had brought home from Bisho. He had administrative paperwork to catch up on, and I was to help him get the statistics up to date before Christmas. Lebrandt began setting up his personal computer and found that he had forgotten an essential cable at the office, meaning that it would not be possible to work on the backlog. His brother might have had a spare cable at his home, but Lebrandt was too upset. He decided to take a seat in the lounge and clean his gun to unwind.

I went to the open plan kitchen which was just around the corner of a wall from the lounge, to make him some tea. It was around 11 p.m., and we were both desperate for some downtime. I switched the kettle on, nattering all the while, got out the cups and heard the gun go off, followed by deafening silence. Somehow, I knew exactly what had happened. I walked around the corner, saw him lying on the floor and heard his labored breathing. He had shot himself in the head.

I called emergency services and attempted to explain how to find our house. We lived in a new complex, so they weren't familiar with it. Becoming frustrated, I gave them as much detail as possible, ended the call and phoned his brother. There was no response, so I decided to call his parents. Lebrandt's father answered. I tried to explain to him what had happened, but he was still half asleep. I then described the scene to my mother-in-law. Shortly after that, emergency services arrived along with Lebrandt's parents and his two brothers. The medical team attended to

Lebrandt. The rest of us stood in the living room in quiet confusion.

The medics could do nothing to save him since the damage from a bullet through his head was too extensive. My husband passed away shortly after 12 on the morning of Christmas day in 1994, nine days before his 32nd birthday at the local hospital. I lost a husband, his parents lost a son and his siblings had lost their brother, the youngest member of their family.

Lebrandt's mother suggested I spend the night with them as the lounge rug was covered in a pool of blood. At first, I resisted, saying that I would be fine to stay in the house. On returning home from the hospital, however, the sight of his blood was too much to stomach. I packed a few things into a suitcase and spent the night with Lebrandt's parents. We sat around in the lounge for a while trying to process what had happened before going to bed. We awoke the next day, still in a state of shock.

I couldn't stop crying. Lebrandt's mother called a doctor for some Bromazepam (an anti-anxiety medicine) after a day or so to help us all. Lebrandt's family managed to hold it together better than I did; someone had to be strong, and, in this case, it was the matriarch of the family. She must have called my brother, Trevor, as he and his wife came to visit me.

I went back home after a couple of days after Harrison and Paul, Lebrandt's brothers, paid to have the lounge cleaned by professionals. My in-laws arranged the funeral, and Lebrandt's sister flew in from the Strand. Before the funeral, the family went to view Lebrandt at the funeral home. His face was incredibly pale, and the morticians had obviously done what they could to make him look as good as possible. I couldn't stay. I took one look at him, turned around and went back to the car. He was later cremated.

My entire family came to East London to support me. This was a difficult time but made that little easier because of my family's presence. The Bromazepam also helped to some extent by largely drying my tears, halting the grieving process for a while - not a good thing as I would later discover.

After going back home, I looked for the bullet casing, but was unable to find it. All that remained from that dreadful night was a mark on the wall and a broken ornament, which had been shattered in his fall.

My brothers and mother stayed with me for a few days after Lebrandt's funeral, and I recall standing at the kitchen window with Keith while washing dishes after a family meal and seeing a girl dressed as a Goth emerge from one of the townhouses below mine. It is strange the things that go through one's mind at a time like this. My brothers left, and my mom remained to support me for a while longer. A detective came around to take a statement, and Harrison and Paul made sure they were there while I read through the statement before signing the document. I had to go to court several weeks later for the magistrate to declare Lebrandt's death an accident.

My tears may have ceased, but I knew I wasn't okay. My in-laws became very supportive in the months after Lebrandt's passing. Despite their efforts, I realized approximately six months later that I needed help. I remember standing at the kitchen sink when I had the feeling that the prayers for all of us had suddenly stopped. There was no evidence on which to base this feeling, but it was too prominent to ignore. For the second time in my life, I made an appointment to see a psychologist. What a waste of time.

I drove to his home office, and the situation was so uncomfortable with him sitting there with a mouth full of potatoes. I asked why he didn't provide any feedback and was told that it was a different form of therapy. Irritating to say the least. What is the point of speaking in a complete vacuum? I might as well have skipped that one, but I tried a second appointment before switching to another psychologist - one who actually responded. Whether the talking helped a little or whether it was simply the passing of time that made me feel more comfortable, I don't know, but those sessions also came to an end. I found talking to my dog Buddy, a Scottish terrier. Far more helpful anyway.

I began working for Harrison in one of his micro-loan businesses in East London. This was extremely stressful and very fast-moving at the end of the month. Harrison had begun this business as a sideline before the industry was subjected to regulation. I think the interest rate on these small loans was around 30 percent a month. I don't particularly recall the precise details. I do know that once insurance paid out Lebrandt's life policy and I invested this in Harrison's business, that my percentage of return was lower than Harrison had arranged with Lebrandt. Whatever the case was, I eventually stopped working in this business. It made a lot of money but also caused enormous suffering for clients because of the high interest rates.

My Datsun had manual transmission, a system that I continually struggled with because of my muscle weakness. As a result, I was unable to stop quickly enough on the way back home from work one day when another driver pulled out rapidly in front of me from a stationery position. I rear ended him. Cell phones had reached South Africa by this stage, and I was able to contact Harrison to come and help me.

He then arranged for me to purchase a Honda with an automatic transmission. I was mobile again, but my walking deteriorated further. I really could not go to town for shopping or anything else without having someone's arm on which to balance. My only solution was to employ the services of a maid to assist me with cleaning the home and to go shopping with me. She couldn't be with me all the time, so going to town and navigating small curbs from parking spots to the pavement in front of shops was really nerve-wracking.

Trevor, Cheryl his wife, and their two children continued to show their support by visiting me at least once a month. It was good to reconnect with family as an adult after so many years apart. Ronald also drove down from Johannesburg with his two children for a holiday break.

For exercise, I found a farm outside of East London where I could go horse riding. Joleen, the owner, ordered an appropriate horse saddle that enabled me to strap my legs down with a belt so that I wouldn't easily fall off the horse. Still, I couldn't do much. Joleen led me around the paddock as I didn't have the strength to remain on a trotting or cantering horse. Amazingly, I did fall off the one day when Joleen's husband Henry was leading the horse. Joleen started screaming at Henry. I hadn't realized these two were married and in the process of getting divorced at the time. I was embarrassed to be caught in the middle but managed to escape unscathed. The same cannot be said for Henry. After the divorce, Henry and I became friends; he went on to marry someone else and still visited me years later after I moved to Pretoria.

In my quest to try and regain some strength in my legs and still not having received any conclusive diagnosis, I also started with water aerobics again.

After Lebrandt's passing, I found myself with more time on my hands. I gave up working for Harrison since the hours were hectic, and I had to ask permission from the gas station next door to use their filthy bathroom. I began to follow up on leads regarding my health and was given a name of a gentleman in Port Alfred who used alternate healing methods. This is how I met Nelson, my second husband.

I arranged for an appointment with him at his home in Port Alfred where he used an external apartment as his office. Nelson had been an electrician at Fort Hare University for several years prior to pursuing alternate healing methods. He studied reflexology, acupuncture, and other similar courses throughout his career in natural healing and developed his own energy healing work in combination with what he had learned and created a treatment technique, which he termed Biokinesis. The term is used today to refer to a method that supposedly can "manipulate the life forces and energies of another, as well as the chemical and cellular aspects of the physical body." I was the one who would eventually fund him to obtain a Ph.D. from a Sri Lankan university for this methodology.

I started to see Nelson for treatments. He then suggested I visit Karina, a friend of his who used crystal energies and guided meditations. On another trip to Port Alfred, I saw Karina for her version of alternate healing. None of these treatments alleviated my symptoms, but my curiosity did introduce me further to the fascinating world of invisible energies. I also discovered along the way that Karina had a crush on Nelson, who was not interested. Instead, he turned his attention to me.

After a few sessions with Nelson, we started going out despite living in separate towns. This was to be the beginning of another long-distance relationship; one that was initially filled with a lot of fun but one that was also to come to a premature end. Because of my personal issues and insecurities, I was a magnet for men who were never going to settle down. It all goes back to the desire to be loved but not understanding what a loving, supportive relationship is. So, I made bad relationship decisions throughout my life. In the end, I have to admit that I really suck at choosing the right partner.

Chapter 9

A Period of Transition

Nelson continued with his work in Port Alfred while I went on with my life in East London. Because my curiosity about his world had been piqued, I took a reflexology class that he offered at a friend's home in East London. I purchased loads of books in the self-healing field, many bought with Nelson on our trips to Port Elizabeth, which had several book shops and a large variety of books on this topic. Having Nelson to guide me through this maze of interesting work was a great help, and I lost myself in a world of energy work, crystal healing, healing with color, sound, visualization, meditation and more. Finally, I had found answers as to how the Christian God with whom I had been raised could be omnipresent, omnipotent, and omniscient.

Nelson travelled down to East London once or twice a month, and I visited him in Port Alfred when he was too busy or broke to come to East London. He was barely making ends meet with his work amid the small population in Port Alfred. Although this was a seaside town, it did attract a more relaxed type of person who was fairly open-minded to alternate healing, but, likewise, the community also contained a sizeable conservative component ensuring Nelson's efforts didn't return a rich harvest.

As a result, Nelson spoke to his friends in East London to access a larger market for his work. He found this improved access through a woman named Wanda. He helped to develop her natural healing aptitude and held classes in groups of five or six people who wished to explore further.

Meanwhile, our relationship grew deeper. Nelson shared a dream he had with me regarding a specific piece of gym equipment, which he believed would be helpful in maintaining my strength. It was quite a mission to source this equipment in the early days without much available on the internet, but Nelson found a company that sold this type of home gym. I ordered the equipment. The home gym consisted of a large board on runners to lie on. I could then set the board at any angle to lie on and push my body weight up and down, using my legs. This was quite an effective tool at the time. Combined with my other efforts to regain my strength, in six months, I noticed that I could lift my foot about three centimeters higher from a standing position. No matter how good my intentions were to continue, I could not help weighing the reality of only lifting my feet three centimeters higher every six months after approximately three hours of exercising a day. Self-doubt crept in. The investment somehow did not seem worth the effort to me at the time and was somewhat distracting given my new romance. Nelson entered my life a little soon for my liking at just 16 months after Lebrandt passed, but being impulsive, I decided to go with it.

Before meeting Nelson though, I reconnected with Delilah from my days in King William's Town. Delilah had always been keen for a party with her husband Charles, who had lost his job and gone on a downward spiral due to his levels of alcohol consumption. Delilah was not too far behind him in this area. Their relationship ended in divorce. I invited Delilah to move in with me in East London. I later sold my Datsun to her since I also owned the Honda. Soon after, however, she moved on.

More changes followed. After Lebrandt died, his father and mother reclaimed the lounge suite, our bed, and a large portion of his clothes. Lebrandt's father arrived at my home with several suitcases and packed up a lot of Lebrandt's clothing. What Lebrandt's father didn't take, I eventually shared with my brothers and kept a few items that had sentimental value. Then his mother demanded to know what had happened to the gems in the ring she had given to Lebrandt for his wedding ring. Lebrandt had taken this ring to a jeweler in East London to melt down to make a wedding ring to suit his taste. The stones had disappeared, and no one seemed to have an explanation as to what had happened to these. Of course, the attention turned toward me. I had no idea since Lebrandt had left me in Gordon's Bay a month or two before going to East

London, which was when he had the ring adjusted in preparation for his return to the Western Cape for our wedding. I suspect now that the jeweler gave him a price to alter the ring, which included the price of the stones. Not that anything I suggested mattered. After leaving East London, I have had little to no further communication with his family, a fact that suited all concerned.

I ended up only with a ring that Lebrandt gave me and some of the home items we had purchased together.

Soon after the funeral, I received a government form to complete so that I could claim a widower's pension. Unfortunately, with Lebrandt's stint working at his brother's fast-food store and the short time that he worked at the micro-loan business, there were no records of his salary to claim anything from this fund. I also had no idea whether I would be able to access his salary records from his previous position or whether I was entitled to but, still in a state of confusion and grief, I let that slide. I would have to be satisfied with a one-time check from his life insurance company and a very small monthly pension from the balance of his insurance. Also, I fought against his youngest brother claiming an insurance policy that he had taken out once Lebrandt began working for him. The details of this are quite blurred but the lawyers who took my case won, which did not make me any more popular with the family. I don't recall how much money was involved, but it represented all I received after Lebrandt's passing. Whatever the case, yet another chapter in my life had reached its sell-by date. It was time to start anew.

I moved on to what I anticipated would be a wonderful new relationship with a new man in my life, new hope in my heart and, eventually, a new town. The Cinderella complex, the white picket fence around a cozy home with a dog and cat beckoned. However, the girlhood dream of having children had long since dissipated. Actually, after high school graduation, the thought of having children never really entered my mind. I felt no loss or deprivation about this issue either since the men I met had children or were past the stage of being interested in beginning another family, all of which suited me. After a decade with Lebrandt, I was now 29. Any new relationship would require building before making any life-changing decisions to include a child. Moreover, Nelson already had three sons, none of whom I had met.

My first weekend sleepover at his home saw us going out and coming back to find a note stuck to my half-unpacked suitcase, courtesy of his enraged ex-girlfriend. That was unsettling, and I returned to East London with the knowledge that Nelson's previous girlfriend was not out entirely of the picture. However, Nelson and I continued to see one another. I buried my suspicions about the possibility of an ongoing relationship between them as I just couldn't stand knowing that one more dream was on its way down the toilet. Essentially, I had just delayed the inevitable but didn't know it at the time and would probably have persisted on this path no matter what advice I received to the contrary. Actually, I did receive negative advice from my mother but because my relationship with her was so unstable, I was not interested in listening to anything she had to say about my life.

As far as Nelson's ex was concerned, I used my sleuthing skills, got hold of her phone number and called her after returning to East London. The discussion was interrupted by a pizza delivery on my side and resolved little. I suspected that Nelson and his ex might still be in the throes of a final breakup and hoped they were no longer sleeping together but the chances are probably good that they were. I ignored this red flag.

I had also ignored a further red flag that popped up the day I met him for a treatment. Nelson had asked me if I was okay with paying the price of his treatment, and I stupidly opened my mouth and mentioned that I had received an insurance payout and could afford to pay. My sixth sense immediately picked up the look on his face. Although his back was to me at the time, he had turned his head slightly over his shoulder and I had seen the mechanisms of his mind working. I knew but ignored the sign. Over time, I managed to fritter away the money, either by funding trips with

Nelson and his further education or by following his bad investment advice.

Finally, I packed up my home in East London and moved down to Port Alfred with my Scottish terrier and Bully, Nelson's large tomcat, who studiously ignored one another. We went about making improvements to his home, including building a new double garage, elegant wooden pathway with stairs and handholds to the front door down a steep slope, installing a water drum and pump for running water to the kitchen and purchasing some decent furniture.

When Nelson returned from Sri Lanka, he gave me a gift and announced plans to work with an ex-teacher to find a suitable location in the area for a free clinic - primarily to serve the underprivileged population. His idea was to provide this service while still taking on paying customers. That seemed like a good idea until, one day, I heard a banging on the door and screaming outside. I peeped through the bathroom door to see what the commotion was about, quickly noticing that Nelson's son, Adam, had the same idea. I was looking through a crack in his bedroom door. Adam had not seen me and closed the bathroom door but not before I noticed an object on the foyer floor. Nelson's ex had gotten wind of my moving in with him and decided to pay a visit. She had thrown Nelson's gift to her through the window next to the front door - the one I had paid for.

The discussion that followed once he returned from work was not pleasant, but I was invested by now and was persistent about this relationship working out or I would get hurt trying. Get hurt I did. Not all of our relationship was bad, as we got to have some fun and see a little more of our world together. It was not an equitable exchange.

Nelson's private practice wasn't exactly thriving either despite his new degree from Sri Lanka, so we had a lot of time to spend together, travel around the Eastern Cape and do some shopping. Whenever we were bored, we would go out for breakfast at a restaurant in Port Alfred or drive a little further afield to Kentonon-Sea or Grahamstown. Getting out and about had become more difficult for me, so I enjoyed his company and exploring the world beyond the walls of home. This is the period where I really got into discovering more about energy fields and human healing, which was always at the forefront of my mind. I still suffered from headaches, although these had diminished quite significantly in line with less stress and no longer needing to commute for several hours while dealing with the monotony of administrative work.

I resorted to using the exercise machine again. Even though I was able to increase the height and the time I spent on this machine, my walking did not improve. Later, I gave this up as a bad job. Besides, I was having far too much fun enjoying life; something that I had not been able to do in quite some time. Bored with visiting local areas, we decided to cast our sights further afield and take a much longer road trip.

Chapter 10

A Time of Travel

We took two road trips, one around South Africa and another that extended into Namibia, the Caprivi Strip, the southern tip of Botswana and Zimbabwe. One of Nelson's sons took care of our pets while we were gone. We took our first journey in 1997. We drove in a Bantam bakkie (Ford pickup truck), outfitted with an obligatory mattress in the back to save on overnight costs. We stopped at camping sites to clean up on our journey. When we got tired of roughing it, we would overnight at a cheap camping site or hotel in remote areas to get some decent sleep and food.

This trip started by taking an inland route from Port Alfred through several small towns such as Cradock, Graaff-Reinet and Nieu-Bethesda. We visited the Owl House, home of the late artist Helen Martins. We purchased an owl (what else?), stopped over at a hotel in Graaff-Reinet and continued onwards towards Namibia. In the Karoo region, we traveled up a winding road around a mountain in the middle of the night. As we topped the plateau, we ended up on a bridge over a dry riverbed, pitted with dry rocks and a crystal-clear full moon shining down. We were so in awe that we had to stop and drink in the view, which was just magical. It resembled a scene from a movie. The moon beams were scintillating; so bright, it seemed almost daylight and close enough to touch, suspended over the horizon. With the shadows playing over the silver-grey rocks, the atmosphere was one of immense tranquility, as if we had inadvertently stumbled on an enchanted land not unlike J.R.R. Tolkien's middle world or that of Harry Potter.

We couldn't stop for long and continued our drive in the early morning hours towards our next destination. We had decided to head for Lüderitz in Namibia. The road was long, and the driving was hot; a few more stopovers, and we arrived at the Namibian border and continued on the long road to Lüderitz on the west coast of this awe-inspiring country.

Upon arrival, we found a restaurant for a late breakfast and began our people watching. Somehow, during our drive to this small town, we had not seen any of the wild horses for which the country was famous. We traipsed down some dusty country roads, lost our way and saw numerous quaint villages in what seemed to be in the middle of nowhere; wondered how the people survived and surmised that some eked out a living in this harsh environment or were employed at one of the many diamond mines in the area. Having had our late breakfast, we drove around town for a while, decided there wasn't much to see except some German colonial buildings and purchased food supplies for the evening. Typically, we bought items to make sandwiches as we weren't really set up for much else.

We headed towards the outskirts of town to find a secluded spot to settle down for the night and found just such a place on the beach. The sun set early so darkness surrounded us; being a distance outside of the town, there were also few lights. After the initial change in the light, the stars shone brightly in the sky. We drifted off to sleep with the tailgate of the bakkie left open because of the heat.

We woke up a few hours later shivering from the cold wind blowing off the ocean. We also noticed strange, stealthy sounds outside the truck; it must have been just after midnight. Nelson got up to close the tailgate. It was too dark to see anything but the following morning he detected what looked to be hyena footprints in the sand around the bakkie. A narrow escape apparently. When we shared this story with friends back home, they mentioned similar incidents when camping, including one involving a hyena that tried to drag a small fridge away from the campsite.

Our finances were stretched thin, so we decided to head back home and save for another trip. Nelson also had to sort out his private clinic as business was beginning to pick up. The owner of a Portuguese café in town had mentioned that she would like a family member from Madeira (one of four islands off the coast of Morocco) to see Nelson.

We headed back home, enjoying the opportunity to travel through Southern Africa and to stop at many of the small towns in the Karoo on our way. Another few months went by with plans for the clinic still being in the pipeline. We saved some money and decided to take time for another road trip before Nelson's business really took off, leaving us with less time to see the world around us.

By then, Nelson had purchased a 4x4 vehicle and added a customized roof rack to fit on top of the canopy. We used it to take an absolutely incredible trip through a couple of the countries to the north of South Africa. He purchased a mattress for the back of the vehicle where we would sleep off the ground in the car. After our close call with hyenas outside Lüderitz, we wanted to avoid giving scavengers a second chance to get too close. We packed the bakkie with whatever we would need. Since neither of us previously had the opportunity or resources to attempt such a trip in the past, we were both excited. It was also good to spend time together without other distractions, and I felt that this would bring us closer together. You'd think I would have learned better by then. Sadly, this was not the case.

We began our journey by heading toward Namibia with no plan as to where we had to be, or what day or at what time. So different from my prior in-laws who would never have considered such spontaneity. Neither did they suffer the consequences of such off-the-cuff decisions as I did. Nevertheless, Nelson and I fully intended to enjoy our trip across Southern Africa. I was not yet using a wheelchair, so we were not challenged with packing space for one. Nelson was tall and strong and easily able to help me physically to negotiate more tricky surfaces and other physical requirements. In rough terrain, he would simply piggyback me to wherever we wanted to go. We stopped at a variety of guesthouses, motels, hotels, and self-service facilities during our road trip, traveling for anything from 6 to 12 hours at a time between destinations.

Our first major stop was at a resort near the Augrabies Falls before continuing on our journey towards the Richtersveld. No internet, no GPS, just road signs to guide our way. I don't think we even had a map to spoil our fun. One of our more memorable experiences on this second trip was when we visited the Richtersveld and stopped at a very rustic camp site with basic facilities. We shared a barbecue with other travelers and spent the night in the back of the bakkie under a very dark sky peppered with silver stars. Just driving around that area of the country was magical as neither of us had seen it before. We enjoyed the area so much that we purchased supplies at a small shop found on one of the many dusty networked roads in the region and camped at the edge of the Orange River after driving through the rough wilderness of the Richtersveld National Park.

The September heat was already becoming unbearable along with the small flies that took every opportunity to try and retrieve moisture from our eyes. The reason why Aussies hang corks from their hats became obvious as that style worked well to mitigate the irritation caused by these pesky critters.

After driving a couple of hours from the rustic camp site and coming over a hill close to the Orange River, we stumbled across a makeshift camp. There were only about three or four other vehicles there. Brief head nods to acknowledge the other parties was the extent of our interaction. Making friends was far less important than cooling down in the river by that stage. Getting into that water was the only way to obtain relief from the heat and the flies and socializing in this remote location wasn't on the cards for any of us.

We packed up the next morning and headed for Ai-Ais, a collection of hot springs situated in the Fish River Canyon in Namibia. Ai-Ais is also located within the Richtersveld Transfrontier Park, which spreads across northern South Africa into Namibia - a dry, seemingly barren area surrounding the Orange River yet hosting a multitude of animal and plant life. Here, we checked into one of the chalets at a resort, enjoyed some good sleep, in real beds after enjoying a refreshing swim in the warm baths. These warm baths were like the Olympic-sized swimming pool that Delilah and I had visited in Aliwal North a couple of years earlier. Because I couldn't go hiking or enjoy any of the other activities, such as horse riding, our stopovers were typically overnight or stretched to two nights.

Our next move was to drive north to get to the Caprivi Strip in the northeastern corner of Namibia. By this time, the two of us had come up with a loose plan to drive further north and then travel eastwards to Zimbabwe and make our way back to the Eastern Cape from there. Traveling through such remote areas, we needed to take some precautions against flat tires and getting stuck in rough terrain. With few towns or shops along the way, we were also often forced to buy food from street vendors or small farm stalls in the middle of nowhere. This was how I came to get my first taste of wild game biltong (jerky).

We came across one such stall selling a variety of biltong and purchased a sample to snack on during the long trip north. I didn't like the taste much, although there was one that I enjoyed but I resolved to stick to beef jerky in the future as that was what my taste buds preferred. It wasn't as if I was averse to trying new delicacies and, with a stomach like cast iron, I knew any unfamiliar foods would not be likely to have a negative impact on my digestive system. However, the memory of my mother's liver dinners was always fresh in my mind, making it easy to avoid the temptation of exotic food items with which I was unfamiliar or the smell or sight of which churned my stomach.

After a few more overnight stops, getting stuck on a sandy beach in Namibia, climbing into the back of the bakkie late at night to get some sleep and stepping on some weird creepy crawlies, we made it to the northern regions of Namibia. From there, we headed east and found a resort by the Caprivi Game Park, located on a lengthy strip of land separating Namibia, Botswana, and Zambia, and touching the border of Zimbabwe. Our travels led us through roads primarily deserted, very bumpy and sandy, which made for slow driving. We were tired, Nelson more so than me since I could not help with the driving. The moment when we saw a sign to a resort, we headed that way with a sense of relief, in anticipation of a good meal and a night's rest on a decent bed and a cool, soothing shower.

Our Portuguese host was very hospitable, probably glad for some more company in such an isolated region. Nelson unpacked the bakkie. We showered, changed into clean clothes, and headed for the restaurant. We ordered Kudu steaks, which were quite tough, and arranged for a river trip the following day. This was crocodile country - creatures I loathe - but our host and guide on the river trip was well-versed in taking care of guests. He brought a picnic basket and took us for a long trip up the river while he and Nelson discussed the border war from the 1960s and 1980s. On our return to the resort, our host was extremely gracious and arranged for a friend to stop by the following day to take me for a microlight flight. Nelson declined his offer and decided to rather enjoy driving around the area on one of the resort's quad bikes. I was determined to try everything new (other than food), that was within my power and resources before my health got to the point where many of these activities would become nigh impossible.

We soon headed toward Victoria Falls. Before reaching this destination, we stopped at a second resort in the Caprivi Strip. This second resort was far better equipped for tourists, much larger and offered more activities. This time, the two-tiered boat was geared for tourists, and we took in the sights of elephants on the shore, glimpsed a few crocodiles from a very safe distance and enjoyed the hippos walking on the riverbanks and around the grounds of the resort, also from a respectable distance. The waiters were incredibly attentive on the boat and in the restaurant. Nelson mentioned that their belief was that disabled people were to be honored. Whether this was true or not, I enjoyed the exceptional service they provided in the brief time we spent there. The next stop was the glorious Victoria Falls, which lived up to our expectations and enthusiastic tourist reviews.

At the Falls, we stayed at a camp site filled with tourists, spent another night in a luxury resort and ended up exploring a local animal sanctuary. Here, I connected with a cheetah and a hyena through the fencing. The animals were brought to the sanctuary to treat wounds or help them to recover from some trauma before being placed back in the wild. I could sense their loneliness and distress despite being surrounded by other wild animals. It seemed they were quite aware that they were not at home and longed for their natural habitat. I saw a similar situation later in Thailand where bears and foxes were contained in small quarters, possibly waiting for larger enclosures to be built. The foxes were literally running up the concrete walls of their cages in frustration, stress, and terror at being locked up in such a confined space. I tried to reach out to the bear through talking to it since it seemed quite tame. However, when it approached me, I withdrew my hand from the bars, feeling like a terrible coward but also aware that this was a wild animal, no matter how familiar it was with humans. I felt like it desperately needed some comfort and connection, but I was unable to provide this. The balance of that sanctuary had massive cages, filled with plants for tigers and a variety of other animals. My hope was that the poor bear and foxes were eventually transferred to a huge enclosure and were happier with their surroundings.

Of course, no visit to Zimbabwe was complete without a sighting of President Robert Mugabe and his over-the-top cavalcade of some 20 luxury vehicles speeding along dirt roads to whatever super important engagement they were on their way to. I found the display of such overt luxury obscene in a country with so much poverty and suffering. The situation deteriorated by 2019, two years after Mugabe resigned, when the country stood on the brink of civil war once again. Such thoughts were far from our minds as we focused on relishing in every moment of our trip, including noticing a meerkat that had possibly been bitten by a snake. We left it in peace to recover since these are hardy creatures, and there was nothing we could do to treat it.

Once we returned to South Africa, we heard from friends how they would take a collection of pencils, pens and writing pads with them when visiting Zimbabwe to barter with locals in rural regions. They had little access to resources and little money, so basic school items were in high demand in the outlying, poverty-stricken areas. We didn't have such items and paid cash for the many ornaments, knickknacks and food purchased along our journey.

Working our way through the country, we also drove to Swaziland and Lesotho to get a taste of the more ancient, indigenous flavors that comprise South Africa. The back of the bakkie was later packed to the hilt with crafts, mohair blankets from Lesotho and handmade ornaments made from wood and sandstone. Because we had purchased so many curios, we had to sleep over in resorts as Nelson was getting tired of unpacking the back of the bakkie to make room to sleep every night. The constant unpacking and packing, especially at night when both of us were tired, was losing its shiny attraction, which was the sign that it was time to go back home. One stopover at the Zimbabwe ruins before crossing the border back into South Africa had added to our load of memories, but our lengthy break was over.

At home, Nelson let everyone know of his return and set about finding a cheap or free building to set up his clinic to treat the local population with alternative medicine. He partnered with an ex-teacher, Astrid, a 57-year-old woman who looked like an Amazon warrior. Astrid had a minute head with a flat, bulldog face atop this muscled body but was, unfortunately, not as cute as a bulldog in appearance or personality. Nelson mentioned to me how she had built a yacht and sailed it to Canada to retrieve her children, which her ex-husband had taken with him without her permission. She had slept with Nelson while she had been in a long-term relationship and charged the clinic customers yearly interest on a monthly basis although she was a teacher and should have known better. Petty of me to describe her in this way I realize but it makes me feel a tad better, especially since she treated me as if I was invisible, something which was becoming increasingly obvious to me. Despite my views, she was quite a formidable, imposing figure who was as jealous and threatened by me as I was of her. In fact, we detested each other.

One incident involved Nelson's son Adam driving me out to the clinic to meet Nelson. On our arrival, I waited for most of the patients to leave before Adam helped me up the few steps leading to the interior of the building. This was my first visit to Nelson's business, and I expected it to be a pleasant one. He had a private room at one end of the building where he saw paying clients and an open-plan area on the other side with several beds where he saw non-paying patients. I knew Nelson was seeing one last private patient for the day.

Adam and I walked quietly through the building, but once Nelson's patient left, we were verbally attacked by Astrid for intruding and invading the privacy of the patient. Adam escorted me back to Nelson's vehicle and left while I waited for Nelson to lock up. He was clearly embarrassed by Astrid's response, and my concerns went into overdrive about their relationship.

Chapter 11

Memorable Moments and the Demise of My Second Marriage

Nelson asked me to marry him once I had moved to Port Alfred, but I refused. I just wasn't ready so soon after Lebrandt's death. However, Nelson was charming, intelligent, and manipulative while I was naive enough to believe he loved me. Our official marriage took place at the Grahamstown magistrate's court on April 1, 1997. Of all days to get married and, yes, I was the April Fool - the joke was on me. He was in it for the little money I had, and I was in it to enjoy some travel time. At least, that is the good part that I took away from this relationship and one that I felt was my second failure after Lebrandt.

Before we were to part amid suspicions, accusations and confirmation of Nelson having an affair, there were a few more trips that took place even though I was becoming increasing uncomfortable in public.

People in the streets and shops would stare at the way I walked. When I dared to join a conversation, many would either speak over me or ignore me completely. I felt as if I was invisible, as if my thoughts and feelings were unimportant. A bit of introspection through the years would indicate that this was potentially because I put everyone else's wants, needs, thoughts and feelings before my own, making them think that I was so strong or so unimportant that this was what I expected and deserved. I frequently seemed to be the one to provide the listening ear and the shoulder to cry on even when I needed that same support. One reason that I don't share much is that it made me vulnerable to more hurt; sharing too much of myself also made me feel even more unsafe.

Over the years, I have found that my chronic disease saps my physical, emotional, and spiritual energy and promotes the chances to make poor decisions based on a lack of self-confidence and limited belief in my own abilities and self-worth. Everyone saw this in me. I cringed in my embarrassment at the weak person I felt I had become - desperate to find love and always looking for it in the wrong places - leading me to become vulnerable to any and every schmuck who was out looking to improve the quality of his life at the expense of mine. I am the true April Fool because, until recently, I kept falling for it.

I had also become the April Fool in terms of the law of Karma. As I mention earlier, I dated several men while Lebrandt and I were going out but living in two separate towns. Then, too, I really messed up a simple task. After Lebrandt had introduced me to his parents on one weekend in King William's Town, where his parents lived at the time, and after we had gotten to know one another, Lebrandt's parents went on a trip. His mother asked me to come to their house to check on their freezer, which was fully packed but faulty. I checked once. However, because I had to walk a very steep hill to get to their house, I needed Marie-Louise to give me a lift. She was not available one day, so I skipped the freezer check. Naturally, his parents came home to a freezer full of rotting meat. I lied through my teeth. I may have barely escaped that one through their modest efforts to build a positive relationship with me.

I tried to come clean to Lebrandt about my cheating on him during one weekend when he was visiting his parents. He could see something was wrong, but I didn't have the courage to tell him. After he moved to Cape Town, I have a strong suspicion that he returned the favor with a colleague. While living in Gordon's Bay, I discovered a healthy supply of condoms in his gym bag one evening. His excuse was that a male colleague had given these to him, but I didn't believe his explanation. Karma obviously came back to bite me during my relationship with Lebrandt and again in my relationship with Nelson.

Thoughts like these made me later wish that I had slept with the horse owner in Grahamstown where I went for a few riding lessons

Janet F. Murray

while still in a relationship with Nelson. The young man had been gorgeous and had made sure I felt every inch of his body as he helped me down off my horse after a riding session one day, but I had resisted his non-verbal advance as I was intent on remaining faithful to Nelson. The last laugh was on me.

During our time together, Nelson and I made another trip to Johannesburg. On the way back, we slept on the plateau of the Baviaanskloof mountains outside of Port Elizabeth. This stop was an enchanting moment that will remain with me for the rest of my life. We had been looking for a safe place to sleep. As we summited the mountain, the sun was just beginning to set on the horizon. Zebras, buck, and baboons dispersed as we came over the rise, our presence clearly having disturbed their reverie and final meals before they settled down for the evening. We parked the bakkie next to a locked hiker's cabin near a small dam and began our own preparations to sleep off the day's drive.

The next day, I awoke as the sun was coming up at about 6 a.m. and was met with the image of a sky covered in what looked like a yellow tennis net. I blinked, closed my eyes again, sure that I was hallucinating and opened them again. No! The yellow netting still covered the sky and slowly dissipated as I became fully awake. This event puzzled me for close to two decades before I came across an article describing a grid of energy around the world. Only then was I satisfied that what I had seen had not been my imagination.

After returning to Port Alfred, we went to visit a friend in Grahamstown. Nelson had been invited by a Madeiran client to go to that island for six months to work there with a view to staying longer. He wanted to eventually emigrate there and spoke about this for some time. Previously, we had made a futile journey to Cape Town to talk to emigration agents and had considered Canada and Australia as destinations, but nothing had come of this effort. Either a bunch of con artists made the offer or Nelson did not qualify for emigration to those countries. Receiving a personal invitation from a Madeiran resident then was like manna from heaven for him.

Our reason for visiting his friend in Grahamstown was to find a home for Buddy, my Scottish Terrier, while we were away with a view to possibly relocating her with this family. His friend eventually agreed to take on Buddy permanently because he had a small daughter who had fallen in love with my pet. The four of us then arranged to stay overnight in a nature reserve just outside of Grahamstown while his wife worked the weekend shift at the hospital. We went in separate vehicles, stocked up on food and barbecue goods for the evening together and set out for the reserve.

The area is extremely rich in history with the British and Germans having set up many forts in the past to fight off the locals in their efforts at colonization. We stopped at what was left of some of the ruins of these old forts in the reserve and found an ideal spot next to a river, enclosed with trees, to barbecue and enjoy being in nature before nightfall. Nelson leveraged me onto the mattress on top of the bakkie for the night. It was impossible for me to climb up there myself as I no longer had the strength to do so. I was about 31 or 32 at the time. Climbing heights or walking without assistance was no longer an option and was becoming worse.

I woke in the depth of the night with this strange sound in my ears. It was as if a wind was whooshing through the trees. I looked around and saw what looked like Hottentots standing in an oval formation in the middle of the day, throwing what looked to be a piece of cardboard, like a crude frisbee, in a type of game. I felt as if I had intruded on an intimate moment in their lives, became scared and must have fallen asleep. Again, I woke up to the same scene but this time I felt their hostility and quickly closed my eyes. I had not intentionally spied on their lives but believe that being in nature allowed me to access a different dimension than was normally possible during daily life. What I saw was not my imagination. I can only surmise that the history of the region and being in nature had something to do with this supernatural experience.

Typically, I love being in nature as it has a very calming effect on me since my daily life is characterized by intense stress. However, these remain two treasured memories as I have always wished my psychic and healing abilities were far more advanced. Experiences like this also show me that I can progress in this direction if I make more of an effort. However, my survival always took precedence as it has to this day, placing this part of my development on an indefinite hold.

By this time, Nelson's twins Adam and Darius were living at the house with us. We then decided to move to Madeira for six months, knowing that the boys would look after Bully and Kitty, our cats, as they did when we traveled. Jason remained in boarding school in East London, and he would stay with his mother and her partner on his weekend and holiday breaks while we were away. Again, we packed up the bakkie and headed towards Johannesburg where we would stay before boarding our flight for Madeira.

It was not a happy time. Our relationship was already starting to break down after less than 18 months together. My mother had warned me against Nelson soon after I had moved to Port Alfred where I had put down a deposit for a house for her to live in, but I was not listening. I didn't want to hear anything bad about my decisions or the man in my life, particularly not from the one person who had dominated my life and judged me for as long as I could remember. I did not have the mindset to hear the positive messages and guidance Mom wanted to share and rejected her advances outright. This situation would continue into later adulthood where the only times we could have a meaningful conversation was when I was extremely relaxed; that seldom happened.

Nelson and I spent the night in Johannesburg with his friends before boarding the plane to Portugal where we would stay overnight while waiting for the next flight to Madeira. We booked into a hotel on our arrival in Lisbon and spent the following two days sightseeing. This was really difficult as the only way to see areas of interest involved a lot of walking. Nelson piggybacked me most of the time, and we took taxis otherwise.

We were both enchanted by the street cafes, the delicious coffees, and cakes, fascinated by the old side of Lisbon with its decorative tiles on old homes and went up a hill to explore an old fort. We crossed the river to see some other site of interest - perhaps not that interesting as I have no recollection of what we went to see - and generally enjoyed the short time we spent there. We soon caught the flight to Madeira and experienced what thousands before us had - a hair raising, short airport runway made even scarier by high winds. Our concerns were misplaced as the pilot was clearly experienced.

Alicia, Nelson's sponsor, met us at the airport and took us back to her home. Her apartment looked like something out of a magazine with the way it had been furnished. Alicia told us that she had come from a poor background on the island and had worked as a housekeeper in the U.K. and U.S.A., which is how she managed to accumulate enough funds over the years to purchase her home and several other properties. I was impressed since a lot of professionals in South Africa would have been unlikely to accomplish what she had with the differences in salaries between first and third world countries. Influenced by her time in the U.K., Alicia filled her home with a classic style of ornate wooden furniture. Everything gleamed with the lush rich tones of natural wood. We had supper, a warm bath and settled in for the night with a cold wind blowing outside, drifting off the snowy mountains in the distance, letting us know that winter would not be over for a few months yet.

The following day was a good excuse to walk around town, or more precisely, for Nelson to piggyback me down the steep lanes leading toward the center of the capital city, Funchal. It was difficult not to compare the streets of Lisbon and Funchal with those of South African cities. Both have statues and some artwork, more so in recent years, but the streets of these older countries were more focused on public displays of their artwork. European influences were also clearly visible in the goods on display in shorefronts. We enjoyed more open-air street cafes, quickly becoming fond of the sweet pastries and delicious coffees they offer. Alicia's cooking had also been influenced by the largely tasteless homecooked colonial cuisine, with the food being overdone and lacking any flavoring, including salt. We found this type of cooking in one or two restaurants on the island and assumed the style catered well to the many British tourists who visited the island. Alicia drove us around the island to get a feel of our environment, took us to outlying rural areas where traditional crafts were popular and cultural restaurants where the traditional *espetada* - outsize version of South African kebabs - were cooked in barbecue style to attract vast meat-loving locals and international tourists.

In the beginning, Nelson saw patients in a spare bedroom inside Alicia's home. Soon, this arrangement came to an end, partially due to the space and privacy issues but also because she and I were beginning to argue. I was alone most of the day in a strange home, couldn't get out and about by myself, and her possessiveness over Nelson's time was starting to irk me. Again, it felt like I was alone. I was being selfish, perhaps, having to share Nelson's time with others, possessive, jealous, too, but his behavior encouraged these insecurities, and he definitely played on these while I desperately tried to get a grip on my emotions and shed the fear of what was daily becoming clearer - our relationship was slowly fading away.

Alicia found a suitable, three-bedroomed apartment close to the beachfront for us to move to and went about spreading the word of Nelson's natural treatment to the islanders. One may have thought this would have provided some more privacy, but it didn't. Alicia was almost permanently in our faces, or more pointedly, in my face. As Nelson lapped up the attention, I became more alone and isolated, and more resentful.

Simply negotiating the short distance between the washing machine in the small kitchen to hang washing on the patio was difficult. I had to struggle with extra weight to traverse this distance with an audience of patients waiting in the sitting room to examine my every move. I could feel their eyes on me as I stumbled along this path backwards and forwards. Eventually, Alicia's sister Irene took over this task as I couldn't face the stares anymore. It was bad enough trying to make a sandwich for myself with everyone following my movements and judging my actions.

I wasn't happy. My attitude permeating the entire household while, Alicia, buoyed by Nelson's attention, increased her animosity towards me. I recall sitting at a café with Nelson once, when she came storming towards me with a parcel, I had asked my mother to send to me. I only had Alicia's address when I contacted my mother to ship me a stock of contraceptive pills, not knowing how problematic it would be to obtain in a foreign country and, for some reason, not having made an arrangement before leaving South Africa. She screamed at me in front of the other people sitting outside the café, accusing me of goodness knows what as she hurled her viciousness at me in Portuguese. I was so embarrassed I had no idea how to respond. She finally marched away, still mumbling under her breath at my perceived abuse of her kindness.

Another time at a favorite restaurant with Alicia, her sister and one or two other people, she complained about my smoking at the table. Having lost any patience with her, I changed places to sit further away from her but refused to stop smoking. She also arranged for Nelson to go and see a patient in an outlying town over a weekend. I insisted on accompanying him. We didn't have our own vehicle so were probably collected by a family member of the patient or Alicia. Stubbornly, I insisted on going with this group, which just made matters even more uncomfortable.

Nelson and I had found a few restaurants we liked to frequent while in Madeira as distrust continued to build a wall between us. One was an Indian restaurant down a very steep hill close to where we lived. The owner was from Kenya, and he mentioned that his wife was from Madeira. Their food was absolutely delicious, and I fell in love with their spicy, flavored tea. Another restaurant served pizzas in a similar style to that found in South Africa, while our favorite on the seafront with an open-air seating served just about everything we enjoyed - other than fish with their heads intact and eyes staring up at me which I couldn't stomach. This last restaurant also served a light beer, cerveza, which I fell in love with along with the vodkas and fresh orange juice. This was where I flustered Nelson so nicely, without even intending to do so.

He had been meeting in Madeira with a young lady who dealt in medical supplies. She bumped into us one evening at this restaurant and started chatting. For some reason, Nelson mentioned something about her being foxy. She had no idea what he meant and, when pressed, he refused to explain further. So, I told her that he meant that she was sexy. Nelson was embarrassed. Unfortunately, so was this lady, which had not been my intention, but his reaction was priceless despite not having a romantic interest in her.

Nelson purchased a wheelchair for me at this stage to make it easier to get around the city. We were heading home after an evening out when we were stopped by some cocky teenagers. They were so confident that they actually stopped in front of us to flirt with me while my husband was pushing me around. That felt good under the circumstances. despite them being a good 10 years younger than me. On another occasion, Nelson was pushing me down the street after we had been arguing and he was angry with me. As a result, he wasn't exactly being gentle or observant. Pushing fast, he didn't accommodate the lip of the curve. As the wheelchair wheels hit this obstruction, I hurtled forward. A bus drove by, filled with locals who stared at me intently. I returned their stare, waved back, and was rewarded with a bunch of grinning faces as Nelson retrieved me from the street and returned me to the wheelchair. I wasn't physically hurt but I purred inside for a few brief moments because Nelson looked like such an ass.

Watching television with friends back home, Nelson had been very verbal about an attractive woman in a movie - not for the first time in real life or on television I might add. I felt that he was being deliberately insensitive. Several other incidents like this took place, where he sidelined me, ignored me and was just deliberately mean. I was a grown woman with insecurities but felt it was cruel to play on these after everything I had given him. Yes, I should have had more confidence. I should not have been so tolerant and forgiving but our time was nearing its end. There was no rescuing this relationship. I had to come to terms with this, but it felt like another abandonment: first by my father, then Lebrandt and now Nelson.

Chapter 12

New Friends, More Travel
and Moving On

At that stage, there were many Portuguese and Madeiran people in Port Alfred and in South Africa, so Nelson found exchanging currencies with contacts was much cheaper than going through the formal route. This is how I was introduced to Alicia's goddaughter, Carmo, who became a friend. Her parents had a café in Pretoria, just a few blocks from my half-sister Miranda's home. We really do live in a small world. I took solace in my newfound friend. We were in a similar position. Carmo's marriage was also failing.

Spending time together, we discovered that we had much more in common regarding our spiritual beliefs and our interests in meditation, energy and so on - our meeting was like finding a kindred spirit. Carmo picked me up to take me out for drives around the island, stopping off at restaurants in the smaller towns outside of Funchal. We did some shopping together, saw a few movies; Carmo introduced me to a favorite beach spot and took us out for a meal at one of the many five-star hotels in the capital. As I was using a manual wheelchair, Carmo was able to fold and lift this into her car boot. I was mobile and strong enough to transfer easily from the wheelchair to the car seat at that time. Because my walking was so limited, our choices of where to go were also restricted, but Carmo went out of her way to make life more pleasant for me, especially as it became increasingly obvious that Nelson had already begun a relationship with someone else on the island.

Being a charmer, he had no problem meeting someone through his patients or even to begin a relationship with one of his patients, which is, I believe, exactly what he did. He also faced no regulations after Madeiran authorities recognized and certified his qualifications.

We argued one evening after Nelson returned from some possibly nefarious excursion with me remaining at the house. Nelson took a telephone book and began hitting me on the face and neck. According to him, this was a method of torture used by individuals in the security industry because it apparently left no marks. He was wrong. Carmo collected me the following day to go out with her and a friend. Although I had gone to great lengths to cover the marks with makeup, the friend later asked Carmo if my partner was abusing me as she had noticed bruises on the back of my neck. This incident, together with the fact that Nelson was going out more by himself in the evenings - were all just more signs that there was no future for us.

Nelson's time in Madeira was coming to a close, and I needed to think about my future. We had discussed returning to South Africa to collect our belongings and that I would return to Madeira with him, but, since this was not going to happen, I had to come up with another plan. I was on the phone to my half-sister in Pretoria fairly often, putting out feelers as to what the potential was for me to go and stay with her after Nelson and I parted. As we would fly to Johannesburg, the idea was to go and sleep over at Miranda's other home in Pretoria before driving back to Port Alfred. I could either move to Pretoria and have a support system in place or move back to the Western Cape where Lebrandt and I had several friends. Weighing my options, family seemed a better bet given my circumstances and the size of the city.

I had spent a lot of time crying in Madeira, living in a miserable relationship coupled with the anxiety of not knowing what the future held. I had been in this dark place before. Still, I hadn't died from this mysterious ailment. However, by then, I knew that my physical decline was inevitable, hastened by emotional stress. It isn't as if I thought much about my future in terms of my physical health since it seemed clear that this disease was chronic and that, one day, I would be totally dependent on others. For the moment, I still felt as if I was able to manage physically.

One evening, after Nelson pushed me back to our apartment, he had to stop at the curb to gather himself when he felt as if he was having a heart attack. It seems he had expected sympathy from me, so must have been disappointed. My tears were drying up fast, as was my interest in the relationship. After flying back to South Africa, Miranda collected us at the airport and drove us to Pretoria, where she had prepared separate bedrooms for us. As much as I had been sharing the circumstances of my situation with her, I wasn't ready for this move. Things were uncomfortable enough, and I wasn't quite yet ready to admit the daunting reality of my life - alone again. Our lives were still in limbo, and I clung to the thought of still being able to rescue what was not healthy for either of us. We stayed at Miranda's home for a day or so before heading to Johannesburg to collect the bakkie and then drive home.

We came home together; Nelson soon left. He had been invited to spend some time in Bangkok, Thailand with a medical doctor. They shared similar interests in healing, and Nelson wanted to pick up some tips and share information. Nelson flew there ahead of me. I met up with him a week or so later. One last international trip; one last fling together, which I enjoyed enormously since traveling alone was becoming impossible. For the 11-hour trips to and from Madeira and a similar time for the flight to Bangkok, I needed to avoid consuming liquid for several hours prior to the flight because, on board, it was impossible for me to get up to go to the toilet. No matter how much information was provided to the travel agent, the more important parts of traveling as a disabled person became lost in translation.

I didn't expect help inflight but did at the end of the trip. I was to be disappointed. I arrived at the Bangkok airport and surprisingly, no arrangement had been made to have my wheelchair waiting and ready for me. Neither had the travel agent made arrangements to help me disembark. The anxiety built as I had to navigate the flight of stairs leading out of the aircraft and then the distance between the airplane to the airport building. I wasn't impressed with the situation but was left with little choice. Eventually, a petite stewardess made an effort to help me down the stairs, and I made it into the airport building where Nelson was waiting. After a lengthy flight, I was dying for a trip to the toilet, followed by a cigarette, and we headed off to find the ladies room and a smoking lounge before going to our lodgings. Nelson had been in Bangkok for a week and had plenty of time to familiarize himself with the surroundings. We were ensconced in an empty student hostel arranged by his connection, which is where we went to unpack.

While there, Nelson arranged for me to have an examination at one of the government hospitals. This was a blessing as I didn't have medical insurance. I went to the hospital, had a blood test, and waited for the results. Apparently, my blood sample was to be sent to a laboratory in the U.S.A. to check for an indication of muscular dystrophy. The results came back after approximately a month, by which time I had already packed up and moved to Pretoria. As expected, the test was negative. My instincts regarding muscular dystrophy were verified. I didn't suffer from this disease and never had. One box was ticked off. The search for answers was still ongoing and would endure for several more years. I exercised this same level of persistence with Nelson. Even though I knew our marriage was over, there was still a small spark of hope in my heart that we would be able to work through our problems. However, that was stifled when Nelson made it clear that he had moved on and done so while we were married. Karma is, indeed, a fair referee along life's journey!

Despite my feelings, Bangkok was an absolute delight. Again, traveling would have been impossible if it hadn't been for Nelson's help and strength. The taxis in this country contained no room to pack a wheelchair. We returned to our old form - piggybacking from one vehicle to the next. We used the tuk-tuks (motorized rickshaws) to get around locally, and taxis to drive further afield to see palaces, reserves and other areas of interest. One such tourist attraction was an elephant sanctuary designed to attract tourists. We bought some bananas, and I was encouraged to feed the elephants. I could see by the way they reacted to me that they knew I was different. Years later, I became more conscientious and would not encourage elephant rides after seeing the volume of information about animal abuses from activists fighting to halt this practice.

Another trip took us to an animal sanctuary in Bangkok where I was presented with the opportunity to take a photo with two chained tigers behind me. Usually up for trying anything new, I declined. The thought of sitting with my back to these two massive, exquisitely beautiful, deadly creatures was not going to be an option. For once, I trusted my instincts. But I then made the mistake of taking a photo with handlers wrapping a python around my neck, which subsequently resulted in a nasty skin rash a few days afterwards, probably from their rodent meals and all the bugs that accompany the secret life of snakes.

Nelson and I also visited an open-air market along the river and sailed up the same river for several hours in a rustic boat, which seated about 10 people comfortably. Our guides slashed the tops off coconuts for us to drink the sweet milk. We partook in street fare, sampling the delicious banana and coconut deserts famous in the city. The taste of poultry though was a no-no for me as were the other proteins on offer: from the small, cooked birds to birds' eggs, frogs' legs, snakes, and other exotic foods to the revolting raw black eggs soaked in vinegar or some such concoction - these foreign delicacies made my stomach turn. I settled for vegetarian fare and enjoyed the slushies made by people who lived on the streets in their makeshift tents. They lived and worked from these meagre shelters, enjoying little protection from the elements. However, the Thai government had provided running water and electricity at multiple points along the pavement to accommodate their needs, which I found to be a novel idea.

We enjoyed the opulence of the palaces; I covered my shoulders to enter the ornate Buddhist temples; we shopped at the markets where the goods were cheap and visited one of the largest luxury shopping malls in the region, incorporating some six levels of a bright, sparkling designer shopping mecca, which was simply too rich for our pockets. A stone's throw away on the overhead electric trams, we found a gem of a shop that specialized in foot massages. They possibly specialized in much more, but we were there to relax. Shockingly, during my foot massage and using hand signals and broken English to communicate, I noticed an elderly lady walk past us, bowed over with her head practically touching her knees as she moved by - mute testimony to the caste society, where the lowly born would forever be enslaved to their "superiors."

We took a tuk-tuk to a massage parlor in a poorer area of the city, where I suspected Nelson had already partaken in the extra services available there. Our trip through the seedy side of the city was characterized by hundreds of stray dogs, many of which appeared to have vaginal or anal damage or disease. I suspected they had been abused, a strange testimony to a society grounded in Buddhism. Around the massive traffic circle close to where we were living, we found a nightclub not far from the foot massage parlor, which had a penchant for Western music. It was a treat to go there in the evenings and listen to Asian people performing karaoke songs by Elvis Presley, Michael Jackson, and other favorites. I enjoyed the club's martini cocktails but had to limit myself due to our budget. A trip to the movies was another eye-opener with the local people standing at the start and end of the film to honor the Thai monarch.

Drives into the countryside included stops at toilet facilities that were mere indented holes in the ground with a drain, which one had to straddle to relieve oneself. This form of ablution was as impossible for me to manage as were the majority of toilets in Madeira where people squatted above the toilet seat to avoid germs but ended up aiming poorly, so piles of excrement landed on the toilet seats. Adaptation had made me an expert in dehydrating in favor of experiencing the world, an obstacle which I believe many others in my situation experienced and managed.

All too soon, our sojourn in Bangkok came to an end. We flew back to South Africa, got in the bakkie, and headed back home to

Port Alfred. My tears had completely dried up. Listening to hour-long calls by Nelson to his new love in Madeira and waiting for him to leave so I could pack up in peace was accompanied by a growing sense of urgency to move on with my life. By the time Nelson exited, he had a few tears in his eyes and was seemingly surprised that I did not.

He kissed me one last time as I lay in bed and headed for the door. The sense of relief I felt at him removing himself from my life was palpable - the final sign I needed to convince myself that I had been enjoying an illusion of love. For some reason, I had purchased a return flight for him on my credit card despite him earning an excellent income. That impulse gesture later came back to haunt me as I couldn't keep up with those credit card payments, subsequently leading to the company taking judgment against me to recover that debt. Nelson and I discussed his return to South Africa to finalize our divorce and that he would make monthly payments to refund me for the renovations that I had made on his home in Port Alfred, among other expenses. I would need that financial support to build a new life for myself. Naturally, he didn't follow through with our agreement.

Ronald flew to Port Elizabeth from Johannesburg to drive me to Pretoria, where I had arranged to live with Miranda, her husband and youngest daughter until I decided the best way forward. I said goodbye to Mom as we left her in Port Alfred with her beloved Alsatian, Suzy, and headed toward a new and uncertain future. I found it just as painful to leave behind my cats Bully and Kitty. Adam and Darius's mother adopted them to live at her parent's farm outside of Port Alfred.

Maybe Nelson and I went on so many trips because he was bored with me. At least, that is part of what he told me following our final break up. That's remotely better than being told I was too fat. After we returned to Port Alfred, Nelson asked me if I believed he had partnered with me for money. By then, I was somewhat wiser and said, yes. Once back in Port Alfred, I thought we would go for marriage counseling and return to Madeira together - but that was never an option. By this time, the insurance money had been dissipated and I was financially dependent on him. As he left, I prepared to drive to Pretoria for my next life chapter.

Chapter 13

Pretoria

Miranda welcomed me with open arms, a fact for which I was truly grateful since she was my half-sister. Miranda and her family occasionally visited us in Port Alfred and called a few times, but we really had little contact. I found that she had organized a bedroom for me, complete with a desk where I placed my computer. I kept myself busy by writing a thesis on color therapy for a correspondence degree from the University of Metaphysics in California (the name has since changed). I completed the work but never received my diploma, courtesy of the postal services. The diploma had been posted to me but had probably gone astray in the changes from the apartheid era to the new South Africa. I attempted to follow up but wasn't successful and left it at that. Even though it cost me quite a bit of money, I knew the degree wasn't going to help me to find a job. Besides, attempting to sort out this postal glitch was not worth the trouble.

I learned to maneuver around the house, balancing against walls when moving from one point to another. By then, I had lost strength in my shoulders, making it even more difficult to get in and out of a bath - courtesy of the emotional stress of my relationship with Nelson. The bath at Miranda's home was especially deep, but I managed. Leaving the house was equally cumbersome since I had to rely on Miranda to store and retrieve the wheelchair from my car. Because of this challenge, going to town alone was no longer possible. The weaker I became, the more my world narrowed. As much as I wanted to move about, I had to exercise patience as Miranda had a family to care for.

Payments from Nelson dried up prematurely after he reneged on his promise to refund me the full amount, I had invested in his home renovations. We had also arranged that he would pay me an additional small sum until I got back on my feet. This didn't happen either or at least, he made payments for a few months but fell short of our agreement. Nor did Nelson return to South Africa for us to finalize our divorce, leaving me a married woman without a husband.

In the years to come, I lightly considered paying for a divorce myself but then felt that I had already invested so much in this man that I would remain married until one of us died. Nelson's failure to pay me created a difficult situation. I couldn't pay rent to my sister, nor could I pay other monthly expenses. I began looking for work in a strange city, in a manual wheelchair, essentially needing help to get to work and back. I still had the car that I had been driving in Port Alfred, which had been modified for me to drive. This was a massive benefit although I still had the challenge of finding a willing helper to remove my wheelchair from the boot.

After a while, I found a job as a phone salesperson: cold calling and selling calendars, desk pads and other items for a charity. We worked in morning and evening shifts at offices in a seedy area of Pretoria. The pay was commission-based. I hated the work. Worse, my success depended on my mood and energy levels on the day. Luckily for me, my colleagues were willing to help me to and from my car, but I still had to hazard public toilets. I managed with difficulty and made a new friend: Anza, a nurse who worked for a national laboratory.

With her help, I made yet another trip to a government hospital for further tests in the vain hope that perhaps some new information had come to light since my last series of tests. Armed with the information garnered from my tests in Thailand, I set up an appointment at the neurological department of the main government hospital in the city. Anza and I headed there early one cold winter morning. I shouldn't have wasted my time (and energy). The specialists were not convinced by the genetic results, clarifying that I did suffer from a form of muscular dystrophy. In the process of testing me physically, one of them became inordinately fascinated by the marks on my feet. I was forced to explain to him that, because my circulation was below par, my bootstraps had made red indentations on my feet, which had remained in spite of a nurse's attempt to heat my legs prior to the new tests. The same specialist asked if he could have the details of the Thai doctor. I initially agreed but then decided to ignore his request as I was so repelled by his lack of perception or outright ignorance.

While in Bangkok, Nelson had acquired some type of steroids for me. I learned to inject myself with the hope that this treatment would improve my strength. However, the shots proved to be another dead end. All my interactions with the medical profession and alternate methods of healing seemed doomed to end in failure. With every attempt I made and every new avenue I followed, I either learned more about another area of healing or ended up being disappointed at the lack of available knowledge. I would withdraw after each failure, renew my inner strength to follow this pursuit or simply vegetate for a while until the scent of something else vaguely promising captured my attention.

I found a place to live in a suburb close to where my sister lived and moved in with another nurse and her two daughters. She worked shifts, and we managed to stay out of one another's hair. In the interim, I kept searching for a better paying position and found a temporary job at a teaching hospital outside of Pretoria as a receptionist/administrator for the neurology division. This was a truly horrible experience. The trip there was long and the roads dangerous, primarily due to unruly bus and taxi drivers. After reaching my destination, I needed to rely on the kindness of someone walking past to help get my wheelchair out of the boot. Once that was accomplished, the hard work began. My arms were weak, so even pushing myself on a level surface was a major challenge. Unfortunately, the path between the parking area and the office involved inclines and rough surfaces until I reached a paved sidewalk.

Again, using the toilet was an issue. For that daily necessity, I would need to exit the wheelchair at the entrance to the narrow room, locking my knees, ensuring my feet would not slip on the surface (a struggle in itself with flat shoes that had sheer soles) and push up with my arms to get to a standing position. Achieving this action also required me to back my wheelchair up against a stable object such as a desk or wall so that it wouldn't move while I attempted this cumbersome maneuver. After getting into an upright stance, I would then edge sideways, balancing against the wall with my hands until I got to the toilet. Then, I would brace my knees against the edge of the toilet seat, push my pants down to the same height as the toilet seat and urinate standing up. Making things worse, there was a window at eye level. Anyone looking in my direction would have been met by the strange sight of a woman standing in a peculiar position in a toilet room. Much to my embarrassment and disgust, one day, a doctor opened the door to watch me doing exactly that. He could clearly see my wheelchair at the entrance to the toilet but was also obviously overcome with curiosity. In the inimitable words of Shania Twain, "That did not impress me much."

I also attracted a different kind of male attention. Declan introduced himself to me while I was shopping in a supermarket with my landlady's daughter. I chatted on the phone with him for extended lengths of time to fight off the boredom in my position at this hospital and was rightfully reprimanded for blocking calls to the department. My relationship, or more pointedly, non-relationship, with Declan would endure for several years. He would contact me, take me out for a lovely dinner at a beautiful restaurant and generally spoil me when we saw one another once every three months or so. A quiet man, who often sat without saying anything for a long time, he had also been a fighter pilot during the border war and was an avid pilot. Later, he took me for a few flights in the small airplane that he had purchased. My relationship with him gave me the opportunity to get out a little and see more of my surroundings but was never destined to develop into anything other than a comfortable acquaintanceship. We were two very different people, and his silences made me quite uncomfortable. At best, we limited our conversations to superficial topics. Nevertheless, he was a highly intelligent, accomplished man, so I was flattered and intimidated by him although he always treated me gently and with affection.

His attention was also a welcome respite from work, where I was desperately trying to get through another stressfully boring day amidst intense hostility from the black staff members. The situation had become so serious in the 1980s and 1990s that a special urban warfare Unit 19 (among others) was created was to manage hostilities between the Zulu and Xhosa factions, which frequently resulted in extreme brutality between them.

Fortunately, even though tensions continues into the 2000s, and while surrounded by this hostility, I received a call to become a receptionist at a national research institute. This was an enormous relief. The organization was in Pretoria, approximately 11 kilometers from where I lived, and was populated by people who were a lot friendlier.

The position meant working in support services for the maintenance department on a large campus, which needed to hire a number of disabled employees to meet national quotas. My colleagues proved to be very welcoming and down to earth. I would have all the help I needed to transfer from my car to my wheelchair. The manager who employed me, quickly realized that I wasn't going to cope well in a manual wheelchair as the reception area was quite a distance from the disabled toilet. Amazingly, they actually had a toilet just for the use of disabled people. Coming from small towns where such amenities didn't exist, I was surprised and delighted.

The manager quickly set about purchasing a power wheelchair for me on behalf of the organization. The next step was to get the mechanical and electrical departments to follow through on this and design an electric hoist to fit on the back of my car. I would be able to store the power wheelchair on this hoist, raise it with a remote control and take it with me wherever I went. Changes were made to the disabled toilet so that it was the same height as my wheelchair, allowing me to seamlessly transfer from the one seat to the other.

Life was looking up. Although I understood that I was primarily a political appointment in the new South Africa, I welcomed the few benefits that came along with this opportunity. This is not to say that I wasn't extremely grateful for the help. However, I also realized that I would become very bored after a few years at this job. In the political climate of the country pre- and post-apartheid, employment of disabled people, especially females, was at the very bottom of the list of priorities for companies. For those who had studied to become professionals, the outlook was far different. For someone like myself who did not have a college degree, I could only be considered for positions such as a receptionist, a saleswoman in a call center or other menial administrative posts. Such positions were more readily accessible and remain a favorite of employers looking to fill their quotas. Illogically, employers seemed to think that disabled people are not physically sound so they must be mentally compromised as well. Equally, many probably considered hiring disabled people as a financial burden considering potential structural changes to buildings to accommodate their needs. Despite these perceptions, I, and many others in similar positions, had to deal with these archaic impressions. Despite my EQ never being up to speed, my physical condition had not impacted my IQ.

I settled into my new position with the help of an elderly lady, fondly known as Aunty Joyce, who was closing in on 70. Her duty was to teach me the ropes so that she could retire. I sat with her at the computer. Later, I was given my own computer so that we didn't need to share. Joyce told me that, between answering a busy phone for the department, I had to record and disseminate maintenance requirements to teams dispersed around the campus via an antiquated intercom system. Technicians had to carry bulky radios around with them in addition to heavy toolboxes and other equipment, a task made slightly easier because they all had vehicles. Different teams were assigned to take care of specific buildings, 50 of which were spread out across the vast campus.

More stress developed in my life as my landlady decided she had to move back to her hometown to keep a closer eye on her growing teenage daughter who had already aborted twins at the age of 13. Her daughter was tall and well developed. Barely a teenager, she looked as if she was 18, a fact that guaranteed boy trouble. We had the obligatory chat with the homeowner, and I went about finding boarders to share the rent. Bill moved in with his girlfriend, Lalula. Bill then persuaded Frank to join us. We still had a shortfall on the rent, so Frank got another friend to bunk with us. The house was old and contained several large rooms and outbuildings. These were also rented out to bring in as much money as possible since none of us had high-paying jobs.

As the years passed, I would find myself wondering whether Nelson ever thought of how I was struggling financially. I had moments of resentment knowing how much he was earning and how I had helped to make that possible. Often, I became quite angry at how someone else was probably enjoying the benefits of his labor towards which I had so generously contributed. Since Nelson never returned to South Africa for a divorce, he effectively short circuited any hope of obtaining maintenance payments because I couldn't afford the legal fees involved in suing someone in another country.

Understandably, scrimping and scraping my way through life financially was tough. I wondered how things would have turned out if I had taken up a stranger on his offer to set me up in an apartment 20 years earlier. This person described me as a butterfly, flitting from one place to another. He had been a lot older than I was, married and lived in another town, so I would have been his pet stopover when on business travels. As much as the financial security appealed to me, I had never been the type of person who could pretend to care for someone if I didn't like him. No matter how good an actress I may have been in my youth, my mood swings would not have coped with that level of stress. Thinking about the possibility and the monetary relief it would have brought, however, gave me a fleeting sense of comfort in those moments when I wallowed in such musings.

Life was not entirely dull. Miranda took me out to movies and shopping at times. I visited her for meals where we would overindulge in wine and laugh up a storm. Our sense of humor was so similar that it was easy to laugh together. It didn't take much to set either of us off after imbibing. One evening, I went to visit her, had a few too many whiskies, drove back home and decided to have a bath to warm up. Big mistake! I had overestimated my sobriety and couldn't get out of the bath. After draining out the water, I lay there for two hours, grateful that I had brought large towels with me and could dry off, get dressed and wait to sober up before attempting to get out the bath. Needless to say, I didn't attempt that stunt again.

Bill was about 35; Lalula was close to 15 years younger. The difference in their ages and maturity levels was the cause of many arguments in the space we all shared, some of which kept the entire household awake in the wee hours of the morning. This communal housing arrangement would also run its course, leaving us all scattering to find alternate lodgings. Mine came in the form of one of the guys at work. He couldn't afford a place of his own and, due to religious reasons, was not prepared to move in with his girlfriend. A devout Christian, he found a house close to his girlfriend's apartment and invited me to join him. As a result, I had a roof over my head and a lift to work and back. This same religious person would later be fingered as one of those who had stolen thousands of rands' worth of electrical goods from the supply shop on the campus where we both worked. On the day I moved out, my Creole earrings also disappeared from my bedroom. I suspect this "pious" individual had taken them to give to his girlfriend as a gift. This incident was quite upsetting as the earrings had sentimental value, having been given to me by my first husband.

Bill and Lalula also found another place to stay and, unfortunately, were subjected to a brutal trauma. Criminals invaded their home, tied up Bill and raped Lalula. She kept her presence of mind and politely asked them to use condoms, which, surprisingly, they did. After this assault, the couple contacted a friend who had emigrated to the Caribbean and moved there soon after. They separated eventually, moved to the U.S.A. where they found new partners and started their own families. The heartache of living in South Africa, with one of the highest murder rates in the world and where rape is often considered a national sport, took its toll on them as it does on the millions who are not able to leave. In a country where fear rules both black and white people via an unrelenting, unfettered criminal element seemingly in control, this is just one further challenge to be faced and overcome in the ordinary lives of everyday citizens.

None of that is related to the end of the hated, racist political system that characterized South Africa for more than a century. For me, apartheid was a non-issue because I wasn't conscious of my benefits and privileges as a white person. Once I was exposed to racism in the workplace, I adapted. On the other hand, when apartheid ended, I quickly became accustomed to being threatened by daily violence, as did most black people. Violent crimes proliferated, with black women being the most vulnerable. From my perspective, the poverty and history of South Africa contribute to this, as does the current ANC government's divisiveness.

A few personal examples of the prevalence of crime will suffice: Ronald and his wife were mugged at the entrance to their gated community in full view of the security guards, who were unable to do anything to help them. Ronald had a gun pointed at his head, while his wife had her wedding ring ripped from her finger. They also lost watches and cellphones. With their small toddler in the car, they were too terrified to do anything to risk his safety. Thankfully, they were not physically harmed but spent several hours in therapy to process this horrific experience.

Not surprisingly, I also fell prey to criminals. As my last boyfriend once asked me, "Who better to take advantage of than a disabled person?"

Once, when sharing a house in King William's Town, I came home to find it had been emptied out. Conveniently, the criminals had access to two or three large suitcases on top of my wardrobe to pack up their unwarranted shopping spree in comfort. Earlier, I had been in the bath with the small windows above me open to the night air. I froze while two male individuals were busy casing the house. I guess it was this inspection that led to the theft as they gained access through the one tiny window that was not burglar proofed and was just several meters off the ground.

Another incident involved the theft of my modified car while my sister, her daughters and I enjoyed a birthday celebration at one of the parks in Pretoria. The security guard had supposedly not seen anything. I marveled at the arrogance of anyone stealing a disabled person's vehicle. Although the modifications were not complex, most thieves would have been hesitant to tackle such a vehicle. I can't blame the security guards as they are typically not well paid. The theft of a vehicle in relation to the potential loss of life in a confrontation understandably created a poor equation for action.

Additionally, I drove an old BMW, which was an attractive option for criminals. Months after it was stolen, the insurance company contacted me to advise that my car had been used in another robbery. I think it was a bank since a fast getaway car was key to the thieves' success. The insurance company wanted to fly me to Bloemfontein to identify the vehicle but changed their minds at the last moment - probably seeing an opportunity to save on travel expenses. They decided to send some miserly schmuck to drive me down to get the job done. This guy was clearly in it for every cent he could make. We stopped at a filling station. His wallet fell unnoticed onto the concrete. I had to fight the urge to not draw his attention to it. Decency won out, and I mentioned it to him. To successfully identify my car, I lost a day's income as I was on temporary staff at the time. I never did get the car back either.

While my experiences and those of Bill and Lalula occurred around 2002 and Ronald's hijacking took place in 2017, such situations had become commonplace in South Africa together with the upswing in brutal rapes and murders, a testimony to the leadership - or more pointedly - the lack of leadership in the country. As the saying goes, "South Africa is not a place for wimps." That is precisely how I feel about living in my homeland, even though the country and its people will always be at the center of my heart. My eldest brother had emigrated to Australia to provide his children with a better life and education, but the rest of us have to learn to live with the poor decisions of past and current politicians and the majority's voting choices in selecting those who they hope will create the least damage and horror for its citizens.

While working at the research institute, I didn't spend much time contemplating politics. My own job had enough pitfalls.

Chapter 14

Independently Dependent

When Joyce retired, I took over her position. The department finally installed software to manage the allocation of maintenance work around the campus. A new black president was appointed to lead the organization, and all receptionist positions were eliminated. This process led to many white staff members resigning, taking financial packages, and being shuffled around to make way for black employees from South Africa and further north, and for other white non-South Africans.

I watched with disinterest. To me, black people are people like anyone else; each of us has his or her own journey to travel.

On the other hand, I leveraged this situation to ask for my own office rather than sitting at the entrance to the building. In addition, I requested permission to study. My request was granted despite the institute's policy that no employee studies would be paid for unless the subject choice was in line with the job. I couldn't help but wonder what a receptionist could study in line with her work. I didn't say that aloud since everyone was fully aware that any further study in line with this job was severely limited, even if a possibility.

Given my earlier attempt to study law 15 years earlier, which ended in failure, I began with a certificate in business management to test my level of self-discipline. To my relief, I had improved. By this point, I was permanently in a wheelchair and could barely pick up a phone let alone a coffee mug. My limitations forced me into using my time far more efficiently. After earning my certificate, I enrolled for a business management degree through UNISA, a correspondence university in South Africa. I gained a few credits for my certificate and started slowly with three modules for the first semester. Once I had passed those successfully, I increased the number of modules to get through the degree a little more rapidly.

At the same time, I met Andy. He came into my workplace, looking to speak to someone from the mechanical department regarding the purchase or renting of forklifts. He was a salesman: blonde, blue-eyed, gregarious, and looked like a Greek god. He asked me out. I declined, saying that I had to study for an exam. We exchanged phone numbers. I expected him to wait until after my exam and was surprised when he called before the end of the day saying that he couldn't wait. I caved in, partly due to boredom. I hadn't been in a relationship for years. I agreed to meet him at a coffee shop, went home and dolled myself up a little and drove out to meet him.

He was willing to help with my wheelchair and get me out of the car. I activated the remote from my seated position. Unfortunately, his foot was in the way of the hoist and landed with some force. His response was very restrained but funny. He then picked me up and placed me in my wheelchair after I lifted the hoist, allowing him freedom of movement again. Having a strong man around to help me with the wheelchair saved me an enormous amount of energy and stress. We enjoyed the evening chatting, eating, and getting to know one another. Andy was very upfront and honest about his past, and we hit it off, agreeing to see one another again. We stayed together for three to four months. He told me that he never started one relationship before ending the one he was in, so I guess it was just my luck that he broke this pattern with me.

We had planned a weekend away together at a resort in Mpumalanga, which ended in disaster. We had argued about something; he had pointed his finger in my face, so close that he removed my contact lens. The problems started because the hotel room doors were narrow. I couldn't get through them to go to the bathroom, so he had to contact maintenance to remove one or two doors. That helped only a little because the entrance to the toilet was halfway across a narrow room, which meant that there was no space to turn once I entered the newly widened doorway. I was so stressed trying to get to the toilet because my feet were soaked in perspiration, making it too slippery and dangerous to stand up. I had to rely on Andy's help and was frustrated and miserable. Naturally, he was not happy either - with the situation and me.

We drove back to Pretoria in silence. With the noises he began making in the following weeks, I knew something was off.

Ronald arranged to meet me for a birthday celebration at a coffee shop in May. In turn, I invited my sister and Andy to join us there. He arrived late and mentioned that he had bought me a birthday present, for which I thanked him although I didn't ask him what it was. His response was to inquire as to whether I wanted to know what it was. He had bought me a microwave, which was needed and welcomed. It was a goodbye gift. The relationship was over. Andy had already started an affair with a receptionist at a doctor's office, despite assertions to the contrary.

Soon after, probably depressed, I decided to leave my job and accepted a position at the institute's call center. While there, I began amino therapy, which also turned out to be an expensive and useless initiative. I likewise took two weeks sick leave, breaking my principle of taking one health day of sick leave a year. This action was met with suspicion because I never looked sick. Actually, I was exhausted, getting up at 6 a.m. to leave by 7 to get to work by 8 but make-up covers a lot more than just exhaustion. The drive to work was a short 11 km from home but most of it involved bumper to bumper traffic. I needed 40 - 60 minutes to cover that short distance. I was also taking six modules a semester and was particularly stressed, which took its toll on my health. I needed a break; my doctor agreed.

I had thought the change to working at the call center would be positive. Instead, the politics were even more prevalent there. No training in the hardware was provided. I had evolved from a highly efficient legal secretary to a glorified administrator. The situation wasn't working out. After a year, I requested a transfer back to my previous job. At least I had loads of time and freedom in between work. My phone seldom rang as everything was managed through the software package.

Nevertheless, I kept busy on my seemingly endless quest to find answers to my health. I made an appointment to see my sister's homeopath. In constant pain, she had developed osteoarthritis after having her children, who helped her get dressed and make meals as she resolved to overcome this challenge. This disease was supposedly medically incurable but with the assistance of her homeopath, a major diet change to vegetarianism and Buddhist meditative practices, Miranda healed herself. She continued with her yoga and was the image of health. Her doctor seemed like just the person who could help me.

Her homeopath gave me a bunch of bottles filled with formulas to support my healing process. None helped. I followed this with massages, reflexology, crystal, and color healing. I found someone who used a computer program and bottles of medicine to test the physical body and treat it. Amazingly, the results from a different software system indicated that I had been bitten by a tick. Now what? Nothing!

I had to relocate for the fourth time during my time in Pretoria. Thankfully, Miranda was there to help. I found a garden flat in the suburb near to where she lived. It had one step down to the bathroom, which was the only drawback at the time. However, the owners granted permission for me to have a ramp installed. The guys at work were willing to help and soon I was rolling up and down the incline. On the other hand, I had no means to transport my power wheelchair to and from work. Fortunately, the guys at work once again came to my rescue and solved that challenge through trial and error. While waiting for them to do this, I struggled with my manual wheelchair for a few days, bought a transfer plank and left my manual wheelchair at home. I was trapped again until they ironed out all the remaining difficulties. The manual chair wasn't stable enough, and the weight of the power wheelchair caused the hoist to bend. I needed a new battery in the car to cope with the motor on the hoist so that it wouldn't drain the car battery; otherwise, sometimes the electrical wiring worked and sometimes not. It wasn't simple to develop a solution, but, eventually, my work colleagues found an answer to that, too.

I had some freedom and independence again. I could drive home with the power wheelchair on the back of my car, push myself out of the driver's seat into a standing position, turn around slowly and carefully and cautiously crabwalk along the length of my car until I reached the back. From that position, I could lower the hoist with the remote control and take a seat in which I felt stable, in control and, most importantly, had sufficient independence to do whatever was on my agenda.

Years passed; many of the colleagues I had known had left. The last survivors of that group stuck together as much as possible. Politics had made work life less pleasant. The whites complained about the incompetence of some black employees and vice versa; one new managerial appointment happily told me how he would get everyone else to do his work once he had reached a sufficiently high enough rung on the management ladder; one woman was fired for racist remarks and another manager was called out for harassing female staff members. Later, there was talk of the finance department not complying with regulations regarding tax payments.

Work continued, although sometimes in strange directions. One female scientist conducted research to determine whether the sun had anything to do with HIV/AIDS. Another scientist publicly voiced concerns about the health status of water and its availability. His views were summarily dismissed as he was working outside of the organization's policies, only to be vindicated years later since raw sewerage was being pumped into rivers further damaging this valuable resource, moving inexorably and inevitably closer to the point of no return. Few scandals rocked the organization though and, overall, it was far better managed than most government departments, being outside the government (a parastatal) and reliant on a mixture of government funding and private income.

I was happy in my garden flat and tried a few maids over the years until I came across Catarina. She worked two days a month for me, helping to clean my small home and shop for groceries, and for fun. My home was so small that I managed to keep it neat and clean enough. Having Catarina come in twice a month was more than enough.

I purchased a washing machine, which was placed in the large bathroom. Since my apartment was the size of a three-car garage, I had a full bathroom with a shower and bath, and a wall separating the tub from the toilet. It was good to have a bathroom that I could move around in without bumping into everything in the process. I was still able to get in and out of the bath with difficulty but had to cope with the situation in the absence of any other solution. I washed my own clothes and by the time the cycle was complete, they were dry enough to hang inside. Catarina changed my bedding twice a month, which was not how I'd been raised, but I was forced to become flexible with my lifestyle and hygiene.

I found a couple of people to form a carpool and help with expenses if not the driving. One day when leaving work, I had an accident, causing more unnecessary problems around finding another second-hand car that I could afford. No one was harmed, but the consequences were aggravating. My brother, among others, helped resolve the problem. I bought an old PT cruiser, transferred the hoist from my BMW and added a stronger battery. It didn't go well. For some reason, the car battery kept failing, resulting in my need to purchase a new battery every two years or less. Something was draining the power. I called an auto-electrician to come and check it out at my workplace. He couldn't find any faults. I laughingly suspected that I was draining the car battery with my temper tantrums in the privacy of my apartment when my exhaustion and frustration levels reached disproportionate levels. There just was no other feasible explanation for the battery needing to be replaced so often and going dead overnight. There was nothing wrong with the starter motor, alternator or whatever other mechanical and electrical functions affected the battery. So, I was forced to look at my own behavior.

The idea was good, but futile. I didn't have the energy to make any changes in behavior. I needed sleep. I needed rest. I wasn't getting enough of either. No matter how much I slept, I woke up tired. I also struggled to fall asleep at night and was restless throughout the night. Sleeping pills weren't really an option for me as I had heard how addictive they could be with side effects resulting in brain fog the next day. My brain was already foggy enough, and I wasn't prepared to take that risk. I also didn't like the loss of control that I suspected would take place if I started taking sleeping pills.

After being able to take eight Syndol tablets a day at times in my 20s with little to no effect, I tried taking a generic version in my 30s, which made me so lethargic that I wanted to stay in bed all day. These tablets contained codeine. I quickly realized I could no longer take that medication as it made me woozy. On the advice of a work colleague, I started purchasing an alternate painkiller, one that combined an anti-inflammatory. It worked, getting rid of the pain without any side effects.

My resolve not to use sleeping tablets wavered when I read about a doctor who gave a particular sleeping pill to a long-term patient that elicited very positive results. The patient had been in a vehicle accident that had left him with brain damage. After giving him this specific sleeping tablet, the doctor reported that he could communicate better and experienced several other health improvements. Impressed and eager to try this option, I contacted this doctor, who had a practice in a distant Pretoria suburb.

His tests required me to have an MRI scan. I got permission from my medical aid and arranged to go to the hospital where this doctor would meet me after the test. Everyone I knew was working so I needed to manage this outing by myself. I drove to the hospital, persuaded someone to bring the wheelchair to the front of my car and headed to the relevant department. Because it was a government hospital, this event was going to involve a long wait, so I took a book with me. Finally, it was my turn to be plunked in a hospital bed and have some procedure done before going for a scan.

After about an hour, a nurse came to see me, helped me into my wheelchair and rolled me into another room. There, I was met by two Muslim doctors, neither of whom were prepared to touch me in order to get me onto the bed in that room. Another male employee was summoned. Some machine was drawn closer to cover my head; I lay there for approximately half an hour after which I was meant to go back to the waiting room. A call to the referring doctor's offices let me know that the doctor was off sick for the day and was not going to be able to meet me. I was annoyed and decided to put this little occasion behind me as another joke. I found another doctor to prescribe the specific sleeping pills, which were meant to be cut in a third and increased to a half a tablet after several days. I tried this treatment for a month. Nothing changed so I gave up on that as well. My instincts told me that nothing would have been accomplished if I continued the regimen. I moved on as I had so many times before.

Coping with a neuro-muscular disease, which was becoming progressively worse, added to my stress and exhaustion. I also knew that the pressure I had put on myself with studying was taking its toll, and I had become noticeably weaker. One day, after arriving at home and parking in the garage, I got out of the car and turned to hold onto the side as I usually did to reach my wheelchair at the back. My legs started shaking. I couldn't move and was frozen in a state of total anxiety and terror. I stood there, knowing that if I fell on that concrete floor that I was going to be badly hurt. After more than 10 years in a wheelchair, no exercise and smoking, my bone density probably left a lot to be desired. I definitely didn't need to add a broken bone to my injury menu. My only hope was that my landlady would come home after work at her usual time. She did, thankfully, and brought the wheelchair to me, which I fell into with a sense of relief. My landlady then told me how her mother had recently moved to an old-age home. My thoughts moved in that direction. I wondered how much longer I would be able to cope on my own and whether it was time to make the decision to find a place that offered some form of help. I was only in my mid-thirties at that stage.

Problems continued. Soon after I moved into my garden flat, I woke one Saturday morning with a buzzing sound in my ears. I opened my eyes and saw a few bees flying around but was too tired to get up to investigate further. Once I did wake up, I got up, got dressed and opened the front door. By then, my flat was filled with bees. I thought they were possibly thirsty so made them some sugar water, hoping to attract them to one spot and figure out what was happening. That didn't help anything but bee thirst. I noticed that they seemed to be focusing on one area in the room. I opened the door of the built-in cupboard, only to find that these little buggers had already built a mud home the size of half a soccer ball.

I called my landlady for help. Like the Keystone Kops, she and her partner arrived armed only with a can of bug spray. The idea was comical, but I was too exhausted to care let alone get up enough energy to laugh out loud. But I was laughing on the inside as they marched in. I blithely watched the looks of surprise on their faces when they saw the size of the nest. Plan B was called for. They eventually located a beekeeper who didn't charge for his services. He showed up soon after, found Madame Queen Bee and transplanted her into a box placed under a tree. Several hours later, the swarm had collected around their leader, leaving the floor of my flat covered in dead little insects.

Another incident in this home occurred one evening during the week when my wheelchair came to an abrupt, unexpected standstill. My predicament called for a superhero: Anderson, a colleague from work, drove the 30 minutes across town with his toolbox in hand. To call him, I had to fall out my wheelchair, drag myself across the room to retrieve my phone and use the remote control to open the gate for him. I couldn't unlock the brakes on my wheelchair to push myself with my feet. Even if I had been able to unlock them, I had no confidence that I would have enough strength in my legs to push myself close enough to reach my phone. I took off my spectacles, fell out my wheelchair and splayed out on the floor - within minutes, I felt a large bump form on the side of my face. It ended up growing to the size of a golf ball as the area filled with blood.

Anderson arrived, and I was able to open the gate. Luckily, I had not yet locked my front door. Otherwise that would have posed a far more complex problem. Anderson found the short in my wheelchair control, fixed it and got me mobile again. My face was black and blue the next day, and I covered it up as much as I could with makeup but there was only so much that I could accomplish. Sitting in my office with the door open over the following days was embarrassing as it looked as if I had been the victim of a physically abusive boyfriend. As with all my previous bumps and bruises, this injury turned green and yellow, subsided, and disappeared.

This incident reminded me of the days when I went to the showgrounds in Pretoria to take my written exams prior to finding out that the university actually offered a special exam venue for disabled students. If I had known about this sooner, it would have saved me a lot of angst. Driving to this alternate venue was much easier; there were fewer people and obstacles to deal with, making life much more bearable in a stressful situation.

Arriving for one exam, I realized that I needed to go to the toilet before heading home. I went to the toilet and found I was too exhausted to do my usual stand-up trick, so sat down. After relieving myself, I discovered I couldn't get up. I had to shout to get someone's attention as I couldn't reach my handbag on the back of my wheelchair. The situation was so embarrassing that I stressed even more while waiting to hear the sounds of another person on the other side of the door. Someone came in, heard my cries for help and contacted building maintenance. The carpenter ended up removing the entire door, allowing a lady to come in to help me. She got me decent enough before calling a man in to help me back into my wheelchair. It took me a while to gather myself and relax before driving home.

Besides this humiliating occurrence, I had written an exam in the same venue only to find that the power was off, and the elevator was out of order. I was on the second floor. The head of the adjudicators didn't have the strength to assist me. No one thought to call the fire department. The next option was to ask the security guard for help. He placed me on the top stair, carried my wheelchair down to the ground floor with the help of the main adjudicator and returned to pick me up to carry me downstairs. Maybe not surprisingly, considering he was a male and the situation, he took the opportunity to fondle my breast while pretending he wasn't doing anything. I remained silent, eager to leave, get home and rest.

After another exam at the same building, I went out to find that my car wouldn't start. Another call to superhero, Anderson, helped me to resolve another mechanical failure.

Later, I discovered that the university allowed disabled students to write their exams at home. As a result, thankfully, the last year or two of exams were written in the comfort of my own home under the watchful eye of an adjudicator. No more traveling stress or rushing to get ready and arrive on time. It took me four and a half years to complete my degree, including honors, and I finished off that chapter of my life in 2011. Did I receive an increase or promotion for my efforts? Not a chance. I was disappointed but had no choice other than to suck it up. Work was scarce, especially for disabled people, other than receptionist/secretarial positions, of course. By that time, however, I was too tired to tackle any further challenges, deal with new buildings, people and traveling. My health wouldn't allow it. I had to come to terms that the boredom of my present position was better than any other option.

Chapter 15

A Diagnosis, Antibiotics, Hemp and More

I heard about an elderly lady named Sonja who was selling some other new potion on the market, supposedly based on nutrients from bees. I tried that for a few months and also experienced no change. She employed several other therapies and brought some oxygen sheets for me to try out. No change. After seeing her for several weeks, Sonja mentioned that she had been to see a doctor in the Johannesburg area. Dr. Donaldson is a British doctor who had made his home in South Africa several decades earlier and is still treating infectious diseases. Sonja gave me his number; I made an appointment.

To see him, I would need to find someone to drive me the 70 km to his practice. Frankie obliged. He was Bill's friend and one of the people with whom I had shared a home after moving out of my sister's house many years earlier. I saw Dr. Donaldson and provided him with a brief history of my health and was sent to a laboratory for blood tests.

When the results came back, I booked another appointment with him to hear about the results. I had a smorgasbord of diseases, including Q fever, spotted fever and chlamydia pneumonia. Dr. Donaldson questioned me about contact with ticks and unpasteurized milk. Suddenly, after so many years of searching, the pieces of my health puzzle began to fall in place. Mom had given me unpasteurized milk as a baby, which was followed by vomiting and a seizure, probably caused by a high temperature. Strike one. I told Dr. Donaldson about nosebleeds in my early years together with severe bouts of tonsillitis. I believe these symptoms were due to the Q fever infection. A full body rash and anemia at 6 when in Queenstown added to the picture together with another full body rash when I was about 11 or 12, which were due to spotted fever and the reinfection picked up by the laboratory; a massive chest infection at 17 and a bronchitis-like reaction soon after starting work at the research organization explained when I possibly acquired the chlamydia pneumonia. Strikes two, three, four and five. All these infections added to my health history. For the first time, I had received a diagnosis that made perfect sense, unlike earlier diagnoses of two separate forms of muscular dystrophy.

These initial symptoms subsided within a few days and were replaced by others over the decades. Besides nose bleeds, tonsillitis, anemia, and full body rashes, the first signs of muscle weakness had appeared when I was about 14 and noticed my right heel catching my left ankle when walking, causing a painful sore. It took years for this weakness to spread further up my arms and legs to my shoulders and hips. In the early days, I found that I could no longer use a stapler as my hands had become too weak. Eventually, I lost strength in my hands almost entirely, making it difficult to pick up basic items such as a coffee mug.

After my time with Nelson, I returned to South Africa and found that the strength in my shoulders had dwindled further, making it more difficult to get out of the bath. To achieve that, I had to push myself up with my hands until my derriere was at the same height as the side of the bath. After that, I could swing around to sit on the edge and shift into my wheelchair seat. The headaches continued to be excruciating and lasted up to three days, with painkillers having little effect. Due to nerve damage, I know that I experienced pain in the rest of my body due to inflammation but was unable to feel it until it worsened to the point that I became extremely tired.

Dr. Donaldson was surprised that I was still able to go to work as he mentioned that many of his patients with similar symptoms were not able to do so and retired. He also expressed surprise that I did not feel that much pain. Because of the brain fog, which impacts my concentration, I struggle to remember to take an anti-inflammatory and pain killer at times. Once I do remember to take a tablet, I can feel the fog lifting and my energy improving. Now, I am able to appreciate the extent of the pain that saps my energy. This is especially true when I am busy and forget that I should take a painkiller. Due to a lack of strength and mobility, I have also only slept on one side throughout the night for years, which can cause pain in my hips and legs.

During 2015, another symptom appeared. I noticed that once I had been in bed for a short while that the front portion of my feet and both hips became numb. My thoughts wandered to whether I might need to have an amputation at some time in the future because of a lack of circulation or just where else this disease would take me. Dr. Donaldson noted how blue and cold my feet became in winter and said that I had Raynaud's syndrome, which is a narrowing of small veins in response to cold or stress. Of course, this situation is not improved by my smoking habit, which also restricts circulation. Winters are typically a bad time as I am permanently cold unless I can sit in front of a heater all day. Once I become cold, I cannot sleep and need up to four hours for my lower legs and hands to become warm again.

Dr. Donaldson explained to me how he had treated many other patients with diagnoses similar to mine. Most of their infections had been recent, though, and only one farmer he had treated had not been able to get out of his wheelchair. I made mental notes of all the information he provided and was uncertain as to whether I should be overconfident or accept the probable reality that I would share the same fate as the farmer, given that it had taken over 30 years of living with these infections before being properly diagnosed. Dr. Donaldson also explained that the human immune system can typically cope with one or maybe two infections but that it would begin to break down with any further bites from infected ticks or fleas and that stress was a strong contributor towards a decline in health under these conditions.

Dr. Donaldson prescribed antibiotics from a family of tetracyclines, which consisted of nine or 11 products. These would be alternated to prevent the infections becoming accustomed to any one of these medications and developing resistance. He also explained, as had the homeopath, that any cortisone used to treat me would have driven these infections deeper into my system. Quinine tablets were prescribed for a month as part of her treatment protocol to help fight these diseases. He warned me against the Herxheimer effect, a short-term response to detoxification marked by a variety of symptoms, including headaches, joint and muscle pain, body aches, sore throat, general malaise, sweating, chills and nausea. Not the ideal cornucopia. I took advantage of this potential and asked him to schedule me off work for a week for every month for the next six months while trying this new treatment.

I cleared this with my boss and looked forward to seeing how I would react to the medications while being able to enjoy some extra rest. As it turned out, the Herxheimer reactions I experienced were moderate, but I obtained a sick leave certificate every month as I was desperate for rest. Mom had raised me to be tough and, I believe, I didn't disappoint her. However, I was exhausted and consoled myself with the fact that I seldom took time off work, other than for my one, self-imposed, health day a year. After my first week of antibiotics, my headaches all but disappeared. I found I was able to wear metal-based jewelry again. I was 38 at the time and first noticed an allergic reaction to metals while in Port Alfred. Any time that I wore a necklace, gold, silver or otherwise, I would end up with several nasty welts on my neck and wrist. These welts were several centimeters in length and approximately a centimeter wide, a little itchy and painful to touch but disappeared within a day or two.

Under Dr. Donaldson's care, I slowly began to feel better. My sleep improved almost immediately although I never felt as if I had enough rest. My energy levels also picked up marginally, which was a relief since I had resorted to taking a food supplement to try to improve this concern. It didn't make much difference, except that I picked up weight for the first time in 20 years.

Dr. Donaldson also warned me about using excessive sugar and supplements, suggesting that these infections thrived on sugar and additional nutrients, increasing their numbers and strength. He further warned me not to eat beef jerky or dried sausage as tick infections could survive in this raw meat. If I couldn't resist eating meat in this form, he said, I should take the precaution of zapping them in the microwave for several minutes to destroy any dangerous microbes.

After spending some 30 years persistently attempting to find whatever illness had stolen my health, I was relieved finally to be pointed in the right direction. I had my answer; I had my diagnosis; now it was a waiting game and irregular blood tests to check my progress. My medical insurance paid for most of this treatment unlike my request for assistance to purchase a new power chair since I would need another in the future. This response left me with a very sour taste in my mouth and was just another insult from the medical profession. How could a board of medical specialists, professionals, highly trained in their field, not be able to diagnose me for over 30 years and then add insult by refusing to pay for a portion of a power wheelchair? This logic baffled, annoyed, and irritated me enormously, but I had to let it go. There were other more important battles to fight, and now, one doctor had given me the tool to do just that.

At first, I started off with antibiotics for one week a month. I had only been on antibiotics once or twice in the past 30 years, so there was little to no chance that I had built up any resistance. After six months, I suggested doubling the dosage in an effort to speed up progress. I was eager to get to the finish line. Intermittent blood tests indicated that my ALS and ALT indicators were elevated, with the laboratory report stating that this indicated early stages of liver disease. Where normal levels should have been at 30 points and under, mine were in the region of 70 to 80 points. Blood tests showed that these levels fluctuated but mostly hovered around the 70-point level.

Dr. Donaldson could not make any promises regarding my recovery but explained that these infections had caused extensive nerve damage rather than harming muscles. The pins and needles in my feet were a consequence of this nerve damage, and the myelin sheath around nerve cells could take up to two years to recover, if indeed, this healing would take place. I don't pretend to understand medical, biological, and chemical processes. However, I could formulate an understanding of a concept within my own framework of personal research. Whether my condition was primarily characterized by nerve or muscle disease had always been a question in my mind. This, too, had finally been explained to me. I now had the information necessary to approach the type of specialist I might need in the future - if at all. Of course, I first needed to develop some confidence in the medical profession and have the cash to fund such a consultation.

I returned to work after my appointment and set about doing what I enjoyed - investigating and discovering. One search led to others as I gathered more information about these infections. Today, it doesn't matter to me as a layperson whether one calls the tick-bite infections spotted fever, tick bite fever, rickettsia, Coxiella burnetii, Borrelia burgdorferi, Lyme disease or any other name. To me, the effects are the same (or at least, similar), which is almost total destruction of health and any concomitant quality of life. If I hadn't become so disillusioned with the medical profession and life in general, I might have been horrified to discover that such a miniscule bug could create such enormous havoc and destruction. If I hadn't become so permanently exhausted from being constantly in survival mode and dealing with the minute-to-minute frustrations presented by the extensive physical disability that these diseases had left in their wake, I might have become angrier in the knowledge that if diagnosed 30 years ago, a simple treatment of antibiotics at the time would have set the trajectory of my life on a totally different path. If I had been given to holding a grudge, I could have blamed my mother for being so neglectful as to give an infant unpasteurized milk.

Naturally, some of these thoughts briefly entered my mind but I was more relieved to have found an answer. My persistence had paid off. I kept knocking on those doors until I found what I was looking for. I had achieved a modicum of success. Only more time would reveal the ultimate outcome of finding that answer. Would it be complete recovery of my mobility, partial recovery, or none at all in terms of my daily life?

The years passed, and I continued to take the antibiotics faithfully every month. Other than curing my headaches, improving my sleep, and marginally enhancing my energy levels, all of which were critical to my quality of life and ability to work, I still continued to become physically weaker. Six years earlier, I had consulted with a medical psychic who had informed me there was nothing wrong with me. Dr. Donaldson said something else. What was I supposed to believe? Was my physical condition perhaps the result of my rollercoaster emotions? I was at a loss. I thought I needed to be patient to uncover further answers one day.

A new tool soon presented itself when I received a call at work. This person probably could not reach me on my cell phone, which was in my handbag hanging over the back of my wheelchair. It was often time consuming for me to get to my phone before a caller hung up. The caller asked me if I knew anything about "brown gold."

"No. I don't know what brown gold is," I admitted.

"Don't speak so loudly," the voice on the other end cautioned. "I met this guy in hospital, and he explained how much this has helped other people to get better." The medicine was known as Rick Simpson oil - angel tears. That call set me off to conduct more research on a fascinating journey.

I purchased Rick Simpson's book online and could barely put it down. Simpson provided a detailed account of his struggles with growing hemp in Canada, jail time, ill health, and healing. I had never been interested in drugs and, like most people, had been raised with the belief that hemp or cannabis were gateway drugs to more dangerous substances. Of course, this product had many negative connotations in society, but I was hooked on just how incredibly valuable its properties were. How could any reasonable individual with a modicum of integrity have hidden the benefits of this plant from society, vilified it and enforced prison time, essentially condemning millions to unnecessary death due to "incurable" diseases or because they didn't have the means to access medical care? I didn't have to struggle to find an answer: Big pharma colluding with ignorant, controlling, corrupt government and businesses. The same thing happens with relentless deforestation and pollution but do these short-sighted individuals care? Not a chance. They don't bear the brunt of their poor decisions; ordinary citizens do. They fill their bank accounts while ensuring that they emptied those of ordinary citizens, in my view.

I purchased some of this thick, greasy, very strong hemp oil containing THC. What I had read about it had convinced me of its benefits. I waited for Friday to arrive as I didn't dare try it out on a weekday. I stuck a pin into the capsule containing the oil, lightly coating the tip to approximately 2 mm and sucked the oil off. Within an hour, my head was spinning. I thought it wise to crawl into bed, very slowly and carefully. I lay down with my head whirling while my mind conjured up all forms of strange thoughts. I became a little anxious but soon fell into a deep sleep. Waking up the next day took several hours. I had never been much of a morning person, and this product ensured that my head only cleared about 24 hours later. This was going to be a challenge to take during the week, but I braced myself. Clearly, I was not going to be one of the lucky ones who could take much larger doses of this oil with little effect.

I persisted and increased my intake very slowly over the next eight months. At this time, I also made the decision to give up on the antibiotics that had been part of my regular diet for eight years. I was 46. My thoughts were that the cannabis would in all likelihood replace the benefits of the antibiotics. It was a natural product and did not have any negative side effects other than making me feel quite sleepy and more relaxed.

Prior to giving up the antibiotics, I had another blood test. This test still showed elevated ALS and ALT results, which were the primary ones that I was interested in as they indicated liver damage.

After taking minute amounts of the hemp oil for approximately eight months, I once again had blood tests done. For the first time in nine years, my ALS and ALT results were within the normal range. Not only that, but there was also no longer any indication of Q fever in my system. I was definitely impressed.

This substance seemed beneficial for so many diseases. If I took enough, it could detox the body, change my taste buds to develop a taste for healthy eating habits and contribute towards my efforts to stop smoking cigarettes. The little that I was able to consume daily destroyed the Q fever in my system and lowered my ALS and ALT levels. I also found that my desire for processed foodstuffs decreased. Chocolates and chips no longer held any interest for me. Further, I had cracked a small bone in the top of my right foot 20 years earlier, which had left a small bump, approximately 1 cm in diameter. Within a week of taking the oil, this bump increased to four times its size and then disappeared.

Rick Simpson's book had been a major eye-opener, incredibly informative and useful. He described cannabis as a sacred plant in his first book. After personal research and application, I cannot help but agree with him. I tried to take the oil regularly and was successful most days. Sometimes, though, I took a break when I felt I needed a clearer head during the week. For some reason, I was very sensitive to the oil and was not able to increase the doses to sufficiently high levels quickly enough for my liking. Consequently, I was forced to stop for a few days. At times I stopped taking it for months, before starting again but this was due to availability and the fact that I had limited success. I also noticed that this product wasn't addictive in the oil form. Not even close. I decided that the only potential addictive quality that might affect some involved its calming effect once the initial dose had worn off. Even that would contribute to healing for those whose emotional states had been overwhelmed by the ravages of disease.

Chapter 16

The Final Death Throes

My dreary work existence continued. Colleagues and friends continued to leave. Eventually, I decided there wasn't much left for me in the maintenance department. I applied to work for the HR talent management division. I had an initial interview with the newly appointed head of this recently created department, a former female psychologist. I thought we would get along well. The paperwork was completed, and I moved to a new building on the second floor.

For the previous three years or so, I lost so much strength that I was no longer confident with my driving. For a couple more years after that, Catarina would help me to turn the steering wheel when navigating around corners as I no longer had enough strength in my arms to do so. Catarina couldn't take over the driving as she didn't have a license. Having her steer was extremely stressful, but I was out of options at the time. Later, when this technique became too dangerous, I once again asked the maintenance guys for help. They arranged for two people to come by my house. The driver would drop off his passenger, Paul, at my home. He would then drive me to work and back home, where he would then get his own lift home with the other driver. This arrangement was not convenient for Paul, not ideal but doable. Paul dropped me off at my new workplace, stopping in the disabled parking bay to retrieve my wheelchair from the back of my car before heading to his building. By now, I had acquired a second wheelchair; one for work and one for home, which did away with the inconvenience of constantly dealing with the hoist that kept breaking down. I was ready to begin my new job.

Unfortunately, the office space we occupied had not been used or maintained for several years. I was assigned to ensure that all maintenance and purchases were achieved to make this space usable. I had requested this transfer because of the promise of receiving new training in the calculation of HR benefits, which I later discovered only took place in Johannesburg. I also discovered that nothing worked in the department. New offices needed to be set up; computers had to be ordered; anything and everything that was broken had to be fixed and painted. New kitchen and office equipment had to be ordered. I was unfamiliar with the appropriate software program. However, as simple as this function was, my manager made the task unbearable by failing to tell me where she wanted certain meetings to be held and kept changing her mind about who should attend and so on. In short, she was deliberately making my life difficult because I was not able to do what she needed me to do at times. I actually laughed about the one manager who I had to include in a meeting 10 or more people, but who kept cancelling at the last moment and inconveniencing all concerned. My new boss couldn't crack a smile about this deliberate sabotage which was, I believed, based on ego - on both their parts.

Navigating all of this inanity was complicated by being able to use the toilet in the disabled restroom, which I found to be totally filthy. All my new HR colleagues were too lazy to walk down the 10 steps to the toilet on the next landing, so they used the disabled toilet, either adding to the filth or inheriting it from the previous occupants on that floor. Either way, I was disgusted that no one had made any effort to report the situation. There were bugs swimming in the toilet bowl and the waste bin was filled to overflowing with sanitary towels and paper hand towels, with flies and midges swarming whenever anyone entered the room. Obviously, too, the contracted cleaning services employee who serviced three floors in the building enjoyed zero supervision and did not care to clean up this area as a part of her work duties.

I really had my work cut out for me, which was a tad complicated since I had to go up and down passages to check on maintenance and still be expected to answer the phone. Unfortunately, I lacked either the extra sensory perception or advanced mental capabilities for that task. I didn't see the point anyway. I couldn't pick up the phone up properly. Besides, all employees had phones in their offices with a message system available via email. In the 21st century, I did not see the point of answering interminable calls, being questioned as to where a certain person was in their office because he or she wasn't answering their phone (my crystal ball is not currently in operation) and then having to send them a message via note or email to respond to the caller's message. Everyone's diaries were also digitally visible and accessible to anyone who wished to contact someone else, so filling a receptionist's position with someone with a degree was just absolute ridiculous in my opinion. This is not what I had expected. I seemed to be dogged by a never-ending series of poor decisions in my relationships and the choices I made in jobs.

This change was supposed to have been positive. My manager also maintained that she would drive me to Johannesburg to participate in the necessary courses. Since my boss was previously a practicing psychologist, I would have thought she would have had a little more insight into the challenges I faced. After all, she had been fully aware of the weeks I had spent trying to explain to the maintenance department what changes were required so I could confidently use the toilet in the disabled bathroom. I attempted to explain that they simply needed to duplicate the heights, distances and so on of the toilet in the previous building in which I had worked. The final result was close, but I still found the toilet seat slippery, and the toilet roll not easily accessible. Because the soles of my shoes were sheer, my feet kept slipping on the floor, making my trips to the toilet extremely stressful as my balance was out of sync with what felt secure.

Adding to my misery was the fact that I had taken an anti-fungal prescription shortly after starting in this new position. As a consequence, the medication destroyed the good bacteria in my gut, leading to constant and excruciatingly painful cramping accompanied by regular bouts of diarrhea. I wasn't a big eater, but this wasn't the point. Every time I needed to go to the toilet, I would have to plan this excursion at least 10 minutes ahead of time to be able to cope with the difficult toilet arrangement. Exacerbating this issue was the fact of constantly having to wait for some selfish, ignorant able-bodied individual to get his lazy ass out of the disabled toilet before I could gain access. I was permanently in tears from my gut cramping despite a high pain threshold and did not understand what was happening to me. I went through copious volumes of over-the-counter medications to stop diarrhea, which is every wheelchair-bound person's nightmare. This lasted 6 to 8 months.

Using the kitchen to make tea and heat food was just one more nightmare in my new work environment. A dishwasher blocked access to the sink and water, so I couldn't fill the kettle. Worse, it was too heavy to use once filled. The microwave did not have a handle or push button for me to open the door as my hands were too weak. At least I was able to open the fridge, although that was not of much use to retrieve the milk if I couldn't make tea for myself. My frustration levels were through the roof. I was crying frequently due to the pain in my gut while my boss was becoming less and less impressed with me. The worse the situation became, the more spiteful and pettier she grew. What was left of my confidence in myself really started to fall apart. My colleagues also began to ignore me or be rude towards me, not understanding what was going on despite my mentioning the diarrhea, pain, and frustration of achieving the absolute basics of not being able to make tea or heat food, never mind struggling with the toilet. There was absolutely zero comprehension or understanding.

I am not the type of person who cries easily, but the cold environment was taking its toll on my physical and my mental health. Not for a moment was I looking for sympathy; in fact, I didn't have the energy to do that, but a little more help and understanding might have been nice. Not having to deal with sarcastic comments or withering looks from individuals who came to my manager's office because she had changed the venue without informing me would also have been nice. However, I got the blame. After all, she was a very important person. I was simply her useless, inadequate minion.

My manager arrived at work one day, using a crutch. She had injured a tendon in her loin and was in some pain. The first thing she did was to get her partner to park in the disabled parking bay to accompany her upstairs. She ordered a couch brought to her office to sit in comfort since it was too painful to sit in a normal swivel chair to work. I heard her rudely telling another manager that she couldn't possibly be expected to go to a meeting at the building next door due to her injury and that the meeting was to be held in her office. Previously, she had no problem in sending me to take care of business at the same building. I tried to carry out her requirements only to find that I was unable to reach the lift buttons as I was unable to lift my arms more than a couple of centimeters. At times, she only occasionally used her crutch to aid her walking, leading everyone to wonder just how much pain she was in. To my surprise, she actually acknowledged or stated one day that I must be familiar with pain and knew what it was like in reference to her own situation. I didn't answer her.

My frustration was on a rollercoaster. At one point, I had become so frustrated with the constant fighting to get things done that I had sent a message to the one maintenance supervisor, saying that he was so stupid that he needed to be reminded to breathe. Of course, this was unacceptable. I was reported. The upshot was that I had to see a psychologist for anger management issues.

On top of this, my manager accused me of being a bully. "You stupid bitch," I thought.

This wasn't a situation that had arisen yesterday, last week or last month. I had been battling with several significant obstacles for an extended period and just kept being ignored. Any normal, reasonable person would have flipped out a long time ago, and she would not have been dealing with intense pain, disability, battling to simply use the toilet in peace and comfort in the process. In any event, I had misdirected my anger to this person and apologized, which he graciously accepted. The two people I should have directed my anger towards escaped and diverted the blame for not fixing my work wheelchair sooner onto the supplier's representative, who lost his job.

At least I had the backbone to apologize for my deplorable behavior. What did my manager do? Nothing but continue to make my life even more miserable. Another manager even had the audacity to ask me how much longer this was going to go on since I had taken quite a bit of sick leave, as if he imagined I was lying or making it up. No insight at all.

I had a few sessions with the psychologist. The results of the report came back that my anger and frustration were completely normal given my physical condition. This psychologist further made it clear that I was suffering from burnout. I spoke to my homeopath and asked him to book me off for a week based on this information. Upon returning, I was required to see the work doctor because of the threat that my burnout posed to the organization. I made a few half-hearted attempts to get examined by the company doctor with the view to being allowed to retire for medical reasons. However, my conversations with him did not produce a positive feeling. He said the process could take up to a year. In my mental and physical condition, I was not prepared to undergo such stress despite the financial benefits this would bring if medically boarded.

My homeopath suggested I take probiotics, which cleared up my gut problem overnight. That was an enormous relief but came too late. I was trapped: unimpressed with the treatment I received with no interest in remaining there for another year while the wheels of the medical boarding process dragged on interminably. If I had remained to see this process through, I believe that the organization would have had to pay approximately half of my salary to me for the remainder of my life, if I never worked in the same field again or until I had recovered from burnout. I couldn't wait. I was done. I had spent 12 years of my life working for this organization, made several friends and had some good times. The institute paid for my degree and a power wheelchair. However, I never progressed to any level higher than that of an administrator, had lost skills, was bored out of my brain most of the time, felt underutilized and came to the conclusion that it was time to move on.

I took a leap of faith as I had done once before when I resigned from the horrible phone sales position without a job and inquired about my pension money. I also asked about the potential for the organization to transfer the work wheelchair into my name. My pension should have been enough to carry me for 23 months, so I signed the papers, was given a farewell dinner and a few gifts and said my good-byes. That day I left early, looking forward to a late sleep-in the following day and enjoying time off to rest and pursue a dream to start a website that I could operate from home and was to be the source of my future income.

Working from home was ideal for someone in my situation but I needed to find something that was viable and would be lucrative in the long term. Despite what I had learned from my business degree and the high rate of failure of start-up businesses, I forged ahead. Not knowing where else to turn, I advertised on a website known for freelance availability in various fields to build the website that I wanted. This website would be named Saffers Mall, with Saffers being the nickname for South Africans, and hopefully would become a popular advertising destination for small businesses, which could typically not afford the high advertising rates needed to increase their branding and reputations.

I was super excited about my new project and got to work posting my project on the chosen site. Soon, I selected a web designer who I thought fitted the bill. We worked together for months. Once the site was almost complete, I spent late nights uploading products to make it look as if it was well-supported. I kept requesting changes, begging, pleading and, finally, threatening my designer, with poor work being the outcome. This initiative cost me a lot of money. Still, the resulting website did not look good for public use. I was running out of money fast and was forced to admit defeat. But, only for the moment. I thought that someday, perhaps, the opportunity would arise again to pursue this dream. Either that or I would have to bury this project. In the interim, I kept busy and entertained with my project, got to stay up as late as I liked and slept until I woke up naturally. I had needed a break, and the rest was good for me.

Catarina continued to come in twice a month to clean my flat, prepare food for two weeks, which was stored in the freezer, and to assist with grocery shopping. From time to time, I would build up the courage to drive the two blocks to the nearby shopping center. Catarina would still turn the steering wheel for me at corners. A stressful trip but it was good to get out. Once I decided that this was becoming too dangerous, even for short trips, I called Charmaine for help. Charmaine - or Dudee as I affectionately called her in response to her calling me Dudette - was Ludwig's wife, a former work colleague. We had hit it off. She visited me on a regular, irregular basis. We shared downloads for entertainment, and she screwed up the filing system on my pc, although her OCD should have guaranteed a perfect job. But she was the type of person who repeatedly misplaced her keys, could talk the hind leg off a donkey and had a very tender heart. In short, my dear friend was an empath. A bit of a crazy one at that.

I was to call on her help again and for much more support. Sitting, relaxing with my tablet the one evening, I received a message on social media from someone named Mac. He wrote, "Who is this educated lady in my Facebook list?" Original or not, this was not the typical half-baked attempt from men at attracting attention or trying to win the attention of a lady. My curiosity was piqued. I looked at my account and realized that we shared a mutual friend, Anderson, my superhero from my previous job. I had only opened a social media account around 2010 and had been a tad suspicious of this platform originally. Consequently, I had not easily accepted friend requests.

I mentioned our mutual friend to Mac, and we started chatting. I was also not keen on beginning relationships on any digital platform after hearing of several horror stories in the news and from friends, so I was cautious about this one, or so I thought. In September 2015, Mac and I continued our conversations online, swapped cell numbers and shared more information. He had lived in the Kidd's Beach area for several years, was from Pretoria and had recently moved to the small town of Piet Retief in Mpumalanga, a couple of hundred kilometers from the east coast of South Africa. Since I came from the Eastern Cape, I was familiar with Kidd's Beach. Over Christmas holidays many years in the past, Mom had taken us camping at Palm Springs, another small resort in the area. We used to wake up at 5 a.m. to walk down to the beach and cross the river for a long walk along the beach front between Palm Springs and Kidd's Beach and enjoy a hearty breakfast on our return. These were magical moments spent with Mom before I became a teenager. I enjoyed fond memories of the area and the times we had spent there, which created a connection between myself and Mac, albeit a loose one.

Mac worked in the security department of a local coal mine outside of the small town of Piet Retief. His background was in the South African Police Service, where he had spent time prior to training for a special unit, focused on urban warfare. After chatting for a month, Mac arranged to drive through to Pretoria to visit me. It was approximately a four-hour drive, and he had little free time, working 12 to 15 hour shifts with two days off every second week or so. The mine where he worked was plagued by unrest from local workers who became violent at times. Not being allowed to carry firearms, the security team had to rely on batons and pepper spray to maintain crowd control. Mac described to me how his colleagues had been held hostage for close to two days by machete-carrying protesters at one point and how traumatic and dangerous the work really was.

I waited for him to arrive, expecting him to reach my address within four to five hours since he was driving at night after a heavy day at work. Instead, Mac needed close to eight hours to reach me, arriving at about 2 a.m. Despite having been raised in Pretoria and knowing the area well, he had also missed a turnoff on the highway, which had delayed his arrived significantly.

We were immediately comfortable in one another's company. He came inside; I offered him a drink. We sat chatting for an hour or so and finally headed to separate beds. We were both tired, he more so than me. I was planning to meet Ronald and his wife later in the day and my mother the following day. Not typical for a new man to meet a parent so soon, but Mom was visiting my sister. If I did not see her then, it would probably be another year or more before the opportunity arose once again. We got up that morning. The cables on my wheelchair hoist were not working, so Mac went to look for parts. After an hour or so he returned, attempted to make repairs but was unsuccessful. Regardless, we headed off to the restaurant at the small shopping center a few blocks away.

We initially met with Ronald and Taliya and their small son. Ronald and Mac seemed to get along well. They returned to Johannesburg. We headed home to catch up on some sleep. On the Sunday, we collected Mom from Miranda's home and shared a meal with her at the same restaurant. Little did I know at the time that, despite our differences, it would be our last meal together.

Things moved rapidly from there. My landlady wanted me out of the garden flat, saying her mother didn't want to live alone after her husband passed away. I needed to move and, being the practical-minded person that I am, it seemed a better option to move in with Mac rather than moving elsewhere in Pretoria only to have to move again to be together. This idea and plan seemed logical to me, and Mac accepted this and found a three-bedroom, two-bath townhouse with a bathroom big enough to accommodate a wheelchair. The townhouse complex was new and in a safe area - as safe as any area in South Africa could be, that is.

I spoke to Charmaine and Ludwig about helping me to move to Piet Retief. I would need someone to drive me down in my car. Ludwig would provide his bakkie and a trailer to move my goods as other means were unaffordable. Catarina and I went about packing up my life in Pretoria for me to move on to the next chapter in my ever-changing existence. It was going to be tough to leave her and other friends and family behind to begin a new life in a small, isolated town far from everyone I knew but the change was now due. In a sense, I looked forward to starting over. I hadn't been in a relationship for a long time, save for a few non-starters since Nelson had left for Madeira, so I also had mixed feelings about the move. What I didn't doubt were my feelings for Mac. We had fallen in love, and I felt compelled to make this decision. The big day arrived. My friends packed up the two vehicles that would take us to Piet Retief. I said my sad goodbye to Catarina, and we set off to begin my new adventure.

Chapter 17

Angels and Assholes

Charmaine drove my car, trailing Ludwig. I felt good to get out of the house since my opportunities to do so were few and far between. We stopped at a filling station and bought some brunch while I phoned Mac for directions. I asked him to have two men to help unload the bakkie once we arrived since Ludwig had a damaged back. Initially, I had difficulty hearing him because the signal was poor. Then, he hung up without confirming his address. He sounded drunk. I wondered aloud if we shouldn't turn around and drive back to Pretoria. I ran the thought past Charmaine even though my options were exhausted. I had nowhere to go if I returned. We drove on with a sense of dread building within me. I tried calling Mac again. No answer. I told Charmaine the limited directions Mac supplied and silently hoped that we would find the place.

We arrived in Piet Retief and, fortunately, located the residence with relative ease. Mac opened the electric gate to let us in. As I feared, he was drunk and had made little effort to find someone to help offload the bakkie. His companion, who had installed inadequate supports in the shower, was equally useless. I started crying, partly in anger that Ludwig felt obliged to help unload my goods with his bad back after I had assured him that Mac would bring someone to assist and partly out of embarrassment at my friends seeing my new boyfriend in this condition. Nevertheless, the job got done even though Mac also turned out to have a bad back, too.

Mac offered Ludwig a beer since he had made sure that he had a good supply on hand before my friends left for the long drive back to Pretoria in the dark. My introduction to my new life did not bode well. My sense of unease grew.

I had taken a massive risk. Lebrandt's death had floored me, followed by a disastrous relationship with Nelson shortly thereafter. As a consequence, I had avoided close relationships for nearly 15 years with only brief encounters along the way. The wounds had never healed entirely, making me reluctant to find a boyfriend. Because of my disability, I had also thought no one would be interested in me anyway. I was at peace with this potential. Mac arrived without warning, and I had truly believed this would be a long-lasting relationship, preferably for life as I was no longer young and had no more interest in foolish games or another breakup.

The house was in a mess with furniture and boxes lying all over the show. I was angry and started crying, again (surprising for me as tears weren't my thing). Despite his drunken state, Mac tried to appease me by driving to get food, since cooking was out of the question. He came back with a burger, placed this on a plate together with a bunch of brightly colored sweets in various shapes. I wasn't hungry but the meal he placed in front of me was so incongruous that I burst out laughing. I could see that he was making an effort to apologize and make amends through his actions. I could not help but forgive him. It would have been churlish not to do so.

Mac hauled me into his bed shortly after that. We were both tired, and I quickly fell asleep. The next day was a mission to begin with unpacking boxes, assembling my bed, which we would need to use since it was the same height as my wheelchair. While in Pretoria, I had ordered a new mattress online, and despite checking the measurements, still found that the feet of my bed were too high. I ended up having to find someone to cut the feet to lower the bed. My first night trying to get onto that confounded mattress in the past had taken several hours and a whole lot of cursing. I had eventually placed towels under the front wheels to achieve more height and endured. In general, that was an incredibly frustrating experience but one that characterized my life. I wasn't keen on repeating that incident, so Mac needed to get to work. It took many more weeks to get our home decent as we systematically worked through boxes. More precisely, Mac busied himself with unpacking my things as I was unable to help him.

By Monday, Mac returned to work, spending between 12 to 15 hours at the mine, coming home and opening a bottle of vodka. His hours were awkward, waking at 4 a.m. to meet his ride to work and arriving home after 6 p.m. or much later. As we spent more time together, it soon became obvious that Mac was a heavy drinker, something I had queried before moving from Pretoria and something which he had lied about. I had heard the clinking of ice in a glass when speaking to him over the phone previously and asked whether he had a drinking problem as I had heard stories of how police force members frequently dealt with horrific crime scenes that severely impacted them emotionally. I hadn't wanted that in my life and, yet here it was.

With the heavy drinking, he also delighted in the sharing of his past memories, from working in a special force's unit, diagnoses of PTSD, anxiety, and depression. Mac regaled me with stories: how he had fought alongside comrades in efforts to maintain peace in the late 1980s and early 1990s during the transition from apartheid to a newly elected democratic government. Images of the brutality of the burning, torn bodies of fellow soldiers and ANC and IFP members filled my brain to overflowing. Mac recalled the figure of a mutilated black woman, posed on a piece of cardboard with a stake through her vagina and a sawed-off breast. She had been tortured by members of an opposition political party, the ANC, according to Mac. This image continues to haunt me; how much more so for Mac, for whom this devastating picture had become an indelible part of his makeup. Through tears of anguish and despair, he told me about seeing his comrades ripped to shreds by bullets and bombs. He described drinking to try to excise these images and visits to porn houses to relieve the utter brutality of his life.

Mac and the majority of his colleagues hailed from the poorest of the poor, broken families, innocent young teenagers after they completed their schooling and easy fodder for politicians and military leaders to place at the forefront of danger. He was, unfortunately for him, an excellent marksman and became a "voorlooper," a front runner or spotter who would go out ahead of the other men to maintain the peace between the ANC and the IFP by terminating the threats that their struggles for power posed against stability in the country.

Accompanied by a partner to watch his back, the two would head out into the dark fields at night for sightings of danger, to counter confrontations between these factions. Mac spoke of invading homes where terrorists or insurgents were said to be located, according to intelligence services. How many people Mac shot and killed was not discussed. In that time, it would have been a futile exercise as his world had become an overwhelmingly brutal cascade of death, cruelty, violence, and hatred. A sensitive young man growing up, he did not envision killing in his future. Poverty and a lack of opportunity had forced him down this road. With every person he killed, a portion of his psyche had been critically wounded. The weight of surviving for so many years in this position while so many of his friends had been murdered in front of him was a burden far too heavy for this tortured soul to bear. Mac mentioned how, during one home incursion, one of the occupants trying to escape death had run down the street in his underwear in the middle of the night, but Mac's superiors gave the order to shoot.

As a result, Mac's emotions were extremely convoluted, impossible for me to separate and even more difficult for him. Mac was focused on an internal horror of images in his mind's eye that were set to repeat in every waking moment and when he managed a few hours of restless sleep. Death hunted and haunted him as he had hunted others.

Drinking and repeating his past became a daily occurrence in our home. I was completely out of my depth when faced with the intricacies of the trauma and addiction that Mac represented. It seemed important for him to share his emotions. So, I listened. And I listened and listened and listened. He was in deep trouble, and I had no clue how to help him.

After a short nine weeks together, he went to work inebriated. That led to a confrontation between him and his boss in terms of company politics and regulation. His manager arranged for Mac to spend three weeks at a Pretoria rehab center that supposedly specialized in the treatment of PTSD, anxiety, depression, and alcoholism. However, as Mac pointed out, he had been down this road before, and no psychologist could help. Apparently, that included psychiatrists armed with their vast collection of anti-this and anti-that medications. No known, effective treatment was available for PTSD, much less so for alcohol addiction, especially when the person in question was disinterested in helping himself. Unfortunately, I was not in a position to grasp the gravity of Mac's helplessness. Only later would it become clearer to me just how broken this man was on so many different levels.

In the interim, I listened to Mac repeatedly recount his past, not being sure whether it provided some relief or just made matters worse. With his heavy drinking, there was also no point in trying to engage in any type of logical conversation with him. Mac spent three weeks at the clinic and returned looking somewhat more balanced and relaxed. Any relief that he had experienced during his time in a professional medical institution soon disappeared as he resumed his job again, with all the stresses of daily work and the regular protests at the mine. These protests inevitably were accompanied by violence, regardless of the reason: salaries, employment of those external to their own communities or because one of the miners had been arrested for some offense. The upshot of all of this upheaval was that Mac felt constantly under threat of losing his life or being significantly harmed physically, which did nothing to maintain his emotional equilibrium.

May rolled around quickly. Mac had mentioned that there were many feral cats at his workplace. I asked him to bring one home. He asked me how he could choose one out of so many. I told him that the kitty would choose him. This is precisely what happened. The one cat followed him around fairly often at work. He had defended the cats from poor treatment by others who were often annoyed by their presence. Mac picked up the cat after work one day, tried to place him in a box for the 40 km drive home but ended up placing him on his lap while his colleague drove. I named him Tommy, a sweet male adult cat who was a bit confused and uncomfortable at being kidnapped and brought to a strange new environment. He had kept company with one of the mine employees who had fed him cat food and pieces of beef jerky from time to time, so he wasn't entirely unfamiliar with people.

My birthday was a week after that and Mac and I went to eat out, leaving Tommy on his own, a situation that he was most displeased with. We came home after our meal to find that he had peed on our bed. The first and last time. It would take Lord Thomas another three months before he was comfortable enough to sleep with us on our bed. After that, he made our home his home and became a member of our small unit. On occasion, Mac would accuse me of loving Tommy more than I did him. At times, I felt the same way but never admitted it to him.

Mac had become even more of a nervous wreck and could barely make it to work sober. We spoke about his circumstances. He then discussed the issue with Janine, his ex-girlfriend who was raising his two sons. She agreed that, if he was not able to cope with the work environment, he should resign. Mac and Janine had lived together for close to 10 years, and she was caring for his two boys after Mac had won custody from his ex-wife who did not sound as if she were equipped to raise them on her own. After spending so much time together, Janine had insisted that Mac leave to find work, and their relationship came to an end, except for her continuing to raise his children. Mac and Janine remained firm friends. He maintained that she was the only person who really understood him.

He stayed in contact with his boys via phone and would later attempt to visit them, an attempt which ended in disaster. In the interim, he resigned from his position to stay at home with the idea that he would look for freelance work in web development and design, skills which he had taught himself and for which he had won a U.K. award for graphic design. Mac was creative and talented, but the years had taken their toll on him, so efforts in this direction to generate an income were intermittent at best. Besides, any income he made was invested in more alcohol.

Shortly before he resigned, Mac had a car accident and wrote off his vehicle but not before being taken to hospital to check his injuries and to have an alcohol test. The hospital messed up his x-rays, focusing on the wrong area of his spine but Mac mentioned that the doctor's examination suggested that the injury he sustained could lead to an early death from a heart attack. Still today, I am not sure whether he lied about this to gain sympathy from me or whether it was true. At the time that he told me this, though, I believed him.

We had only been living together for six months. In this short time, I developed an inkling of how our time together would pan out. Miserable was the word that came to mind. His uncle also passed away during this period. Due to a lack of finances, we decided that it would be difficult to attend his funeral. I was surviving on credit cards and a paid-up insurance policy. I sold my car to help pay our rent. Two of my brothers were able to help us cover a couple of months of rent too, while Mac continued to drink away whatever funds we could accumulate. Once he received a modest pay out after he resigned, Mac decided the money would be put to good use by visiting his sons, who he had not seen in four years. I agreed.

In July, Mac bought an airplane ticket, which seems logical enough but for a fatal flaw: Mac feared flying. He left early enough to make sure that he got to the airport on time. Several hours later, I received a call from his friend's wife telling me that Mac was in jail for the second time in the space of a few weeks. He had bought a bottle of vodka before leaving Piet Retief and had pulled off onto the side of the road, supposedly after narrowly missing a collision with an oncoming vehicle. Mac had then driven into Ermelo and stopped at a filling station; the state police had been called, and he had been taken to hospital to test his alcohol level. A female officer had noticed the bottle of alcohol lying on the passenger seat and had laid into him, beating him with her fists and screaming at him.

Mac said that he had remained calm throughout and had gone to the hospital willingly. He didn't have much choice: he was handcuffed at the time. While there, the female officer continued to heckle him until he finally lost his cool, freed himself from his handcuffs (cable ties) and head butted her. She went down like a stone and lay there dazed while additional security personnel were called to manage the situation.

After the hospital incident, Mac was incarcerated at the local police station. He sat there with murderers and rapists as he had done in Piet Retief. I was frantic trying to get some help for him as the officers refused to get his medication out of the car to keep him calm. I was also concerned that rough handling would damage his back further. While there, the street-smart Mac had managed to arm himself with a sharp piece of prefabricated material that he had acquired on route to the police station or in the police station. Mac explained how two prisoners had tried to attack him in the cell. In the struggle, he cut the one in the thigh and the other across the chest. They were both sent to hospital. No one saw anything.

Being in a space with criminals presented further challenges as Mac and his fellow inmates bore witness to two other male prisoners having sex. Another was trying to increase a gap in the ceiling around a light. Being in a helpful mood, Mac gave him further direction on how to do the job, climbed through the roof himself and convinced the security guard to open the gate as he had been given permission to go out. As smart as he was, Mac was also incredibly lazy. He walked to a nearby café, purchased some Coke and cigarettes and nonchalantly returned to the police station through the front entrance and asked to be let back in his cell. This he did after confronting the female officer by asking her what had happened in her life that she hated men so much. He clearly touched a nerve as it was apparent from the reactions of the male officers that they had knowledge of her past. He came home not having seen his boys, not knowing that he never would again.

Within my first six months with Mac, I had asked for his help to turn my failed website into one that worked. He adjusted a previous site that he had created to meet my requirements. While advertising, I had a response from a Canadian to go into partnership with us; Mac would need to copy the site and adjust it for this market, and we would draw up an agreement regarding profit-sharing. My dream had not yet died, or so I thought. However, Mac was not up for the job. I had to let this dream go into hibernation a second time, angry in the knowledge that the Canadian would already have hijacked our idea and started his business without us. A little effort on Mac's part and our financial struggles would probably have been over in another year or so, but life, and Mac, had other ideas. I carried on plugging away at my freelance writing while he did what came easily to him, self-medicating in the form of alcohol.

Times were difficult while I desperately searched for work online. Anything would do for me as long as it brought in an income. Searching for work on one freelancer site was a nightmare, as jobs were poorly paid. I realized too that there was little recourse to recover monies owed from the employers on the site. Finally, towards the end of November 2016, I struck gold. I found a website that required academic writing for students - essentially writing their college and university assignments for remuneration. This was a foreign concept for me and not a route that I would have taken during my studies, but I was grateful to finally find a means to generate an income and one that I could accomplish from the comfort of my own home. Even though I could pick and choose what assignments I wanted to work on, the hours were brutal, and the pay was mediocre although much higher than similar websites, some of which paid only $3 for 300 words.

My work began in earnest in the month of December, and I quickly also found myself working 12 to 15 hours a day to keep us afloat. Because of the difference in time zones and locations of customers around the world, I would frequently work until 3 am and get up again three to four hours later to work on the following deadline. The number of hours I chose to work was in my control but the time I worked was dictated by our expenses. I didn't earn enough to cover Mac's financial responsibilities but was able to pay for the household and cover my own. While doing so, I had to give Mac my credit cards to do grocery shopping, a situation which he took full advantage of as only an addict can. I was still making excuses and justifying the situation at that stage as I believed I loved Mac and he needed help. Even though I had never had children and don't really think of myself as being a nurturer, I was definitely empathetic about his health issues and the obvious physical and emotional pain he endured.

Eighteen months later, Mac moved into the second bedroom. With my work hours and his difficulty in sleeping, it was no longer feasible for us to share the same bed. The only way I was able to get into bed was if it was unoccupied. Neither did I think that it was fair to wake Mac in the small hours of the morning after he had finally managed to fall asleep. Because of his health issues and more pointedly because of his drinking, his liver was overloaded with toxins as was the rest of his body. In a resting position, his blood pressure levels were typically around 140/190. His heart was working at the pace of running a marathon while he was lying down. Waking him unnecessarily would place undue pressure on his health, so sleeping in separate beds was the only logical option as far as I was concerned as I needed as much rest as possible between deadlines.

Shortly after arriving in Piet Retief and with all the drunken drama in Mac's life, I took the opportunity to look at his phone messages. Something was out of sync. I quickly realized he wasn't being truthful with me. Invading someone's private phone was not my style, but I was compelled to find out what was going on with Mac's work, his drinking, going to the clinic for treatment and so on. There, I discovered that he had remained in contact with an old high school girlfriend. Nothing wrong with that per se, but the content of these messages alarmed and angered me. Essentially, he was cheating on me emotionally. Of course, he ducked and dived and finally apologized and assured me it wouldn't happen again. Yes, it did, but he placed passwords on his phone, so I had no way of checking from then on.

Our lives settled into a routine of me working almost constantly, and Mac walking to the shops to do grocery shopping. He did most of the cooking. When he didn't, I ordered takeout or asked him to also buy food for me when he was busy maxing out my credit cards at the booze shop, right next door to a café and across the road from a fast-food shop. When angry with me, he made sure he bought food for himself and not for me. It would end up in the toilet anyway as he couldn't stomach a large meal on a body soaked in alcohol. I continued to listen to his stories of woe and misery and finally became tired of this repeated tune.

No matter how much advice or support was offered, Mac had an immediate reason as to why this or that suggestion would not work and would not benefit him in any way. He began going out late at night, bottle in hand, to park somewhere outside the home and drink in quiet when our arguments became too much. At such times, he would walk out in the middle of the night and leave the back door open and/or unlocked, knowing full well that I couldn't close or lock it, often needing to call a neighbor for help to feel safe. This was a bone of contention for me as Mac had spent time in jail for drunken driving and had come home to share stories of the criminals he had encountered in the police cell. He was fully aware of how physically vulnerable I was and despite knowing the extent of rapists and murderers in the area, still left doors open (not just unlocked) in the middle of the night.

Our relationship wasn't all bad. After his first trip to a Piet Retief jail cell, I gathered enough money for the anticipated bail, but the magistrate let him go pending receipt of his breathalyzer test. I went to the magistrate's court accompanied by our house cleaner with the expectation of paying bail. I found he had been returned to the police cell and headed in that direction to meet him. Mac was grateful for the effort I made to support him and expressed his thanks. We were still in love if you could call it that.

That was a momentary spike in our relationship. Mac celebrated Christmas day, New Year's Eve, Valentine's day, and birthdays alone while I remained a sometimes silent and always frustrated observer to his foul behavior. I realized that I was responsible for choosing my circumstances and accepted the pain and misery while awaiting until the opportunity arose for us to go our own ways.

Worse, around then, Tommy also suffered an injury. We suspected that an angry neighbor had kicked him while he was courting a lady cat as we did not have the finances to have him castrated. One day, he arrived home from one of his forays, unable to place any weight on his left hind leg. A trip to the vet and x-rays showed that a bone in his heel had been broken. He would need to go to Pretoria for an operation. As serendipity would have it, I had made enough extra money in November 2017 to be able to arrange to pay for someone to take him to Pretoria, wait for the doctor to complete the operation and bring him back home. I was like a mother waiting for her child that day. He returned home at around 9 p.m. that evening with medication to prevent infection and for pain. Instructions from the doctor were to keep him inside for six weeks to allow the pin in his heel to set. In addition, Tommy had been castrated by the same vet.

We had a very hot December, but Mac had no interest in keeping his windows closed or helping me to change the litter box. I couldn't handle that on my own or do anything with the windows. Tommy may have been missing a favorite, fun body part but his hormones were yet to fade. Before his heel had a chance to heel, he made a run for it to find whatever female cats were in the area. Mac was also meant to take him to the local vet for weekly checkups to ensure that no infection had set in, but even this task was too much for him. I had to make peace with the situation and hope that Tommy healed properly and would be able to use his left leg without discomfort. Today, he has healed well but cannot bend his left heel because of the titanium pin. As a result, his movements have become restricted, which has affected his hips to some degree. Other than that, a bit of a sensitive digestive system and the cold that complicates his life a little during winter, he is happy and comfortable. My faithful, furry little companion has continued to be a source of immense comfort and joy to me. Incredibly enough, he would later save my life.

Mac and I might have loved each other, but that wasn't sufficient. He took me for granted, stealing, lying, and cheating. I collected boxes with the idea to pack up and leave but the truth of the matter was that I couldn't afford to move and still hoped that this relationship could somehow be saved. I had taken a huge risk moving in with him, traveling far from family and friends; I had needed a place to stay and had honestly hoped to sort out my finances before moving in with him but now felt as if my choices were limited. Karma again. I had moved for both love and survival, and Mac had lured me in for the same reasons. Our foundation for building a relationship had been weak at best but hope lived on. I wasn't yet ready to admit to another failure in this area of my life. Mac called me Angel; I had my own pet name for him.

As our arguments heated up though, I found myself becoming someone that I liked even less than before, except now, I no longer enjoyed the peace of being single. Mac's behavior worsened substantially after giving up work. Our lives together became a minefield of disappointment, accusations, and rage. He was behaving like a total jerk. Our relationship changed me to the point that I was doing the same as my hopes were dashed against the rock-hard world of survival, a demanding mistress who sucked the joy out of life.

Just as Mac needed someone to pay while he slowly drank himself to death, I had needed a soft place to land. His street smarts were leagues ahead of my naivete. Eventually, decades of deceit, charm and entitlement won out. Mac got his way, and I was left feeling used; a failure and determined not to allow this to happen to me again. There would be no winners in this battle.

Chapter 18

Endings and New Beginnings

Early August 2017, Trevor called so say that his wife had passed away from cancer. Her struggle had lasted several years. Due to the distance, I had not realized just how serious her health issues had become. I was still living with the impression that she would pull through. This was the 21st century after all. They had two beautiful children and had enjoyed a long life together. With both children out of the home, Trevor would have his own long healing process to go through. More bad news followed several months later.

Early in 2018, I received a call from Ronald. He mentioned how he had just spoken to Mom, and she seemed to be speaking another language. Mom only spoke English and Afrikaans, so this news was very disturbing. Ronald and the family had arranged for her to move to an old age home in 2017 because she hadn't been coping physically, had lost a lot of weight, and fallen several times over the years. As difficult as it was for her to sacrifice her independence, we all believed she needed care. None of her children - especially me - were in a position to provide this in their own homes. Ronald arranged for Mom to live in an Alexandria care facility, sharing a flatlet with a younger woman. Mom was 83. She prided herself on her independence and enjoyed taking extended walks on the beach, but this period of her life was over. Mom lasted a few months there and then insisted that she would be better off in Grahamstown, where she had previously spent a short time at an old age home. This didn't last long either with staff members preventing her from leaving the premises and accusing her of being aggressive towards them and others in the facility. Mom was moved back to Alexandria and was then placed in the shared residence since no flats were available. This was the same old age home where her mother, Bessie, passed away.

I phoned Mom after my discussion with Ronald. The supervisor had to call her from her room to speak to me at the front desk. I was concerned because she sounded as if she was speaking Dutch of some other foreign language, but I was unable to make sense of what she was saying and what was going on. The home called for an ambulance the following day to take her to hospital in Port Alfred. Attempting to call there to hear about her condition and progress was difficult with one of the nurses simply disconnecting me. Rough handling had made Mom miserable as she had injured her scapula in December 2017. She was in no mood or condition for further ill treatment. Ronald, Trevor, and Robert arranged to go down to see her and make their own efforts to find out what was going on. Discussions with Keith and his wife, Andi, in Australia, resulted in Andi querying whether Mom was on the correct meds for Alzheimer's or dementia. Andi worked in the medical industry and knew that some institutions continued to prescribe outdated medication for patients, which only worsened their symptoms. Mom's medication was changed but it seemed too late to help her. We suspected that she had a mini stroke; her speech was affected as was her physical mobility.

Our only option after Mom returned to Alexandria was to ask staff members to use their phones so that we could speak to her (or at least have some level of contact) via video calls. After all, she was not in a good place and needed as much support as possible. I was not in a position visit, living over 1,000 km's away. After a similar, second health scare later, Keith travelled from Australia to visit Mom, sort out her medication and ensure that a local doctor was called regularly to check on her health. Unfortunately, we weren't able to see one another due to the logistics of my getting to Alexandria. Keith's budget and time were constrained, preventing him from traveling to see me either. His focus was on spending as much time with Mom as possible and ensuring that she was as comfortable and taken care of in the absence of any of her children being available to assist her. We all had to be satisfied with the situation in the absence of alternatives.

We spent the majority of 2018 staying in touch with Mom. Trevor and his new girlfriend Mandy collecting Robert in Grahamstown to visit Mom once a month to keep an eye on her health and to provide emotional support. These months were disconcerting as none of us knew whether the next health scare would be the last or whether Mom would rally again. With everyone being spread so far geographically and being busy with our daily lives, we all made efforts to keep in contact via video calls. We kept each other aware of the situation by posting comments on the WhatsApp family group. Mom landed in hospital two to three times during 2017 and 2018, with my brothers providing video access to speak to her during those difficult times and offering a level of support. It was incredibly difficult to see this once proud woman looking so vulnerable. Mom's incredible sense of independence and her spirit for adventure were behind her, a fact which was difficult for us to process and more so for her as she entered the last phase of her life.

In the interim, I was getting on with my daily workload and trying to process Mom's health status while coping with Mac's drinking and concomitant bad behavior. There were brief respites like Mac getting drunk and doing a naked dance in the middle of the night. These transitory moments when we allowed some love to shine through were interspersed with suicide threats and attempts, one of which resulted in my calling a neighbor for help to have Mac committed at the local hospital for treatment and observation. Again, this was a temporary measure to save his life. After two days I was missing him terribly, knowing that he would have been going stir crazy in the hospital in the new South Africa where infrastructure and service delivery were falling apart before our eyes. It was worse for Mac as he was a silent witness to the failed outcome of a new democracy; a powerless observer of what he had fought and sacrificed himself for along with so many other young men who survived to become breathing shells of their former selves. Political corruption and greed by the previous party in power and the current ANC led by the rampant, blatant theft of Zuma and his cronies had won out with the worst of human nature having come to the fore. Our neighbor collected Mac from the hospital and brought him home.

Mac continued with his drinking, managing to stop for a week or so on a few occasions. We barely spoke anymore as I focused on writing deadlines while he busied himself with graphic designs and creating two to three websites in the time that we were together. He had received a small inheritance after his uncle passed away and had purchased a second-hand car from a friend. He also lent some of his money to this same friend, who had a reputation for being very tight with money. Mac had been drunk when he agreed to help him out, and we both wondered whether this friend would pay him back.

To keep himself busy, Mac also spent some time chatting to the neighbor's brother, Sipho, and drinking with him in his garage on occasion, despite knowing Sipho was not a very nice person and despite the suspicion that he had murdered someone and gotten away with it. Mac was a former police officer, so I had some respect for his thoughts in this regard. This same neighbor had also tried to provoke Mac by running behind him in the open area of the townhouse complex, pointing at him and shouting that Mac was a *boer* (a farmer). As Mac explained, calling him a *boer* was not an insult but a compliment, which was beyond Sipho's comprehension to understand, whether stoned on hemp or sober.

On the day of this incident, I was so sick and tired of Mac's behavior and that of the neighbor, who played his mindless, repetitive, doef-doef (electronic) music constantly that I was ready for some entertainment. Mac had frequently told me that he was a very good fighter, and I wanted to see evidence of this myself. I went outside to observe Sipho trying to provoke Mac. Another neighbor who had a furniture-removal vehicle outside with several assistants witnessed this ongoing show, much to their amusement. Sipho's young friend and his own son were laughing at his antics, clearly thinking that he was going to get the better of Mac.

Sipho sat on the steps opposite our townhouse. I asked him why he didn't hit Mac while he was drunk. Sipho clearly had wanted to do so for a long time. I was enjoying this because I knew he would come off second best. Maybe, a good beating would bring a swift end to their childishness.

Mac was at the other end of the complex standing with another *boer* neighbor at the time. He headed back in my direction, wanting me to go inside to safety. I was annoyed as I was enjoying the show but missed the climax. I had egged Sipho on. He approached Mac again after I was inside. I heard a thud. Mac had connected Sipho's chin with his left fist. Sipho went down, bleeding a bit from the mouth. On the plus side, the incident appeared to have shocked him back into a state of sobriety. There were no hard feelings after this as both men knew they had been behaving like idiots. Mac also suspected Sipho of stealing loose change from his car, which was entirely his own fault as he never bothered to lock it and the garage stood wide open for anyone to help himself. Nevertheless, our relationship with these neighbors remained strained as they were loud, which interfered with the little sleep that Mac or I were able to get on most days.

Another incident occurred at this neighbor's house, which really shocked us and the other residents. Mac and I awoke around 2 a.m. to hear loud voices coming from their garage. We heard the sound of bottles being broken and wondered if they had started a party on their return home. We heard Sipho's sister speaking in a very even, calm tone, clearly giving orders in Zulu, which we couldn't understand. They were holding a kangaroo court in the middle of suburbia. We were shocked but reckoned that their victim possibly deserved a beating and did not interfere. A loud crack made it clear that whoever they were beating had taken a hit to the head, whereupon the bottle broke, followed by silence. Mac was up and peeping through the curtain so that I could receive updates. They had dragged their victim out of their garage and left him in front of a house closer to the main gate and proceeded to clean up the blood. A while later, we heard a police van arrive and the victim was taken to the police station.

Not wanting to appear too obvious, Mac waited a few days before getting the lowdown on what had happened that night. Apparently, our neighbors had been at a nightclub. On their way out, three thugs had attempted to hijack their vehicle. Our neighbors narrowly avoided the theft. After arriving home, our neighbors decided to go back and see if they recognized their attackers. They found one and brought him back home for some bush justice. After beating him, they carried him out and dropped him in front of another house and gave the police some other feasible story about this thug attacking them at the gate entrance. He was a violent criminal, so no one was too concerned about the neighbors taking the law into their own hands in a country where anarchy was fast becoming the norm.

Other than collecting boxes to pack and move myself, I also battled emotionally with the additional pressure I was under regarding Mac's health and behavior. I had been prepared to help him, but his attitude was so destructive, towards himself and towards me, that life for both of us became a matter of survival. Neither of us were going to escape this situation unscathed. I called family members when I began to have thoughts of suicide, unfairly placing stress on them in an effort to be heard. Life vacillated between eating well or starving, depending on how Mac felt about purchasing food next door to the liquor store during his daily visits. He continued vomiting on a regular basis and made several trips to the doctor for blood tests to check his liver function and to acquire repeat prescriptions to manage his health, none of which helped much as the excess alcohol negated everything else. He was addicted as was his abusive, alcoholic father, who had committed suicide soon after Mac finished his schooling.

The passing of his mother added to Mac's grief as a young man as they had shared a close relationship, particularly because his father had often smacked his mother around although Mac had been too young to prevent this violence. Mac had also fallen prey to a predatory male family member as a young boy. Adding to a dicey upbringing, Mac married a school sweetheart who later cheated on him with his best friend, leading to their divorce and Mac fighting for custody of his children.

A life of abuse culminated in one too many traumas, leaving Mac incredibly fearful of death. His period in the special unit of the SAP had been extended, giving him the reputation of an old man because he had survived so many of his peers, an unusual achievement by all accounts. The smell of burned bodies haunted his days and nights, and special training for an advanced special unit saw him break a bone, which brought an abrupt end to his ambitions. His ex-wife's betrayal was the last blow to his sense of self and existence in a harsh world. Mac gave up trying a long time before we met and had forgotten how to live anymore.

While struggling, Mac purchased his friend's car. Once the going became tougher towards the end of our relationship, he packed his vehicle in June 2018 and walked out the door without a word. I thought this was the end, finally and enjoyed a few days of confused peace, not knowing where he was or what he was up to. My question was soon answered when I received a call from him. He was in Pretoria; he said he had needed a break and would be heading back soon. On his return, I questioned him further, being very suspicious about whether he had visited the woman he had been in communication with from before we had started dating. He had seen her, and he returned to Piet Retief without his electronic notebook. This was the fourth personal computer that he had gone through in our time together. I surmised that he had pawned this one for cash, while the others had been destroyed by being drowned in alcohol, including my spare pc.

Mac had returned and so had his usual lifestyle. While sitting in the lounge soon afterwards, I heard a strange gurgling sound coming from Mac's room and wondered if this was an attempt to gain my attention or if he was in trouble physically. I rolled to his room to find him lying on his back, his hands shaking and him gargling for breath. It seemed as if he was having some kind of seizure. I asked him if he knew his name and knew who I was as he appeared disoriented. He looked at me and called me by his former wife's name. I wasn't sure if he was joking or trying to get a rise from me. Mac's mouth was full of blood. I thought he must have bitten his tongue, which accounted for his difficulty in breathing.

I attempted to persuade Mac to go to the hospital, but he was having none of it. I then called the neighbor once more to ask him to take Mac to the hospital. He came over, willing to help but Mac didn't want to get out of bed. I lost my cool and told him to stop being a narcissist and go to the hospital. Finally, he gave in and went to the hospital, where he was kept under supervision for a couple of days and provided with new medication for depression and anxiety.

Mac came back home. While he was in town one day, my sixth sense told me to go into his room and look at his notebook. His WhatsApp messages were open on the screen. I looked to see what communication he had recently with his Pretoria floozy. I wasn't disappointed. On seeing the exchanges between the two, I got stuck in and sent both of them my own messages, liberally laced with toxicity. I knew that Mac had his phone with him and would be seeing what I wrote. Of course, as expected, his support was for this woman. He dropped everything to return home, probably after first calling her to assure her of his undying love and support.

I was enraged. I had supported him for two years and put up with his awful behavior while barely being able to get out of bed in the mornings - literally. When I asked for help in this respect, it was given so reluctantly that I had resorted to throwing a temper tantrum or struggling for over an hour to get out of bed. Getting into bed was difficult but doable; the opposite had become a major problem for me, sometimes successful and other times not depending on my energy and strength levels on the day.

No matter how much support I gave him, it hadn't been enough and, clearly, never would be. I had made many sacrifices for this man, and he couldn't even help me out of bed. Further, I had paid to have his car fixed after returning from Pretoria, paid for a lawyer to keep him out of jail for his first drunk driving charge and kept a roof over his head. Despite this, he had felt justified to lie to me, steal from me and cheat on me. I was angry. I was so angry that by the time Mac returned from town, my anger had transformed into a deadly silence. My patience and tolerance boundaries had been breached one last time. That fragile spark of decency, gentleness, and goodness in him was blinded into obscurity by this rage.

He came in, sat down on the side of my bed, and had the temerity and arrogance to ask whether I was happy with the damage I had caused. I moved to the lounge to get away from, not wanting to see him or hear anything further he had to say. It was at times like these - there had been several in the two-and-a-half-years we had spent together - that I longed for my mother. Despite our past differences, I longed to be able to speak to her for some comfort and ask for her advice. Now, it was too late.

Mac came through to the lounge a while later, sat down in his chair and began telling me in a hysterical voice to stop what I was doing while holding his legs. I retorted that I wasn't doing anything, but he insisted that I was practicing some kind of witchcraft, which is why he was experiencing shooting pains in his legs. It occurred to me that this could have been because of the seizure I thought he may have had earlier. Before I could respond, he ran out of the back door. By this time, I had zero patience left and decided not to follow.

A couple of hours later, another neighbor came to me to ask if I knew where Mac was. She told me how he had jumped into someone's car at the entrance to our complex, screaming about me practicing witchcraft on him. Not knowing what to do, they had taken him to the police station. Once at the station, the police had apparently also not known how to respond either since no crime had been committed. So they released him.

Mac came back to the complex, but I had locked the doors. He ran up and down outside for a while, knocked on other neighbor's doors and carried on as if he was in a combat situation. I called security, not feeling at all confident or comfortable about letting him inside. Security arrived and placed Mac in handcuffs while he continued to go berserk, telling them to look at how I was moving the curtains. I was moving the curtains in an attempt to see what was going on. One security guard asked if he could come inside to get water for Mac. I let him in. He got water for Mac, and I gave the guard Mac's cigarettes and his medication, warning them that he was capable of escaping his handcuffs. Of course, they didn't believe me, feeling confident that they were armed. They drove Mac to the police station where he spent hours screaming in rage before releasing him the following day.

I received a call from Mac the following morning asking if he could come and pack up his belongings. I confirmed that he could come around if he was accompanied by his previous manager and friend as I wasn't comfortable being alone with him. Mac came with his friend and spent several hours packing his goods into his car while his friend and I waited in discomfort and making small talk in an effort to speed up the process. Mac looked exhausted but was calm. He completed what he had to do, and we said our farewells. By this time, there was no more animosity left between us - just pain, grief and the sense of loss that came with the breakup, and a longing for what might have been. Mac finally drove off, leaving me alone in the home we had shared.

This was the first time in little more than two years that I had been alone. I felt a sense of isolation - a massive contrast to how I felt when I had lived in Pretoria alone. Unfortunately, I had also experienced a sense of isolation in our home and loneliness on the occasions when Mac closed me out while taking or destroying what he could. It was as if he didn't want to see me happy or succeeding in my work endeavors as this highlighted his own situation and sense of hopelessness. He also was not prepared or capable of making any effort to improve his circumstances. Mac was clever. Taking the easy route out of difficulties had become a habit for him, combined with the fact that he had given up trying a long time ago.

I asked Mac where he was going. He said he didn't know. He had many friends and former colleagues and a sister in Pretoria, so I wasn't too concerned about his lacking any plans. His friend, Barry, still owed him money and knew that Mac had moved out. My hope was that this would give Mac some leverage to persuade him to pay back the money, which, in turn, would keep Mac going for a while. I went inside, made myself some tea and sat in silence, mulling over the past few years while wondering about my own future.

Chapter 19

The Struggle Continues

Mac remained in contact with me after he had moved to Pretoria, sharing news of his visits to the same woman he had been speaking to while in a relationship with me. He mentioned that he found her cold as if I had any interest in his extra-curricular activities with her. He called several times, often late at night when he struggled to sleep. Sometimes, I answered his calls. Other times, I ignored him - dependent on my writing deadlines, mood and whether I felt able to deal with his intoxicated ramblings. Mostly, I felt relief that he had left and was grateful to have some peace return to my life, if only for a while. We had forgiven one another for the damage done, but I remained sensitive to his abuse caused by his addiction, whereas Mac seemed impervious to the effects of his destructive behavior on others.

With Mac gone, it did not take long for Sipho to take advantage of the fact that there was no longer a man in my household. Working at my computer one day, I heard loud voices outside and eventually went out to see what was going on. Sipho and two friends from the townhouse complex had taken it upon themselves to sit outside my garage door, citing the fact that they were cold and following the sun. They had brought empty crates with them as seats and were sharing a beer while smoking and leaving their cigarette butts and matches lying around. I told them it was fine for a short while and then lost my cool when they were still there several hours later in the shade and had been joined by another of their frequent visitors. Realizing they were taking advantage of my situation and less than impressed with their sexual suggestions, I told them to bugger off. Their arrogant, opportunistic behavior was soon to take on a more sinister twist and one which I thought had somehow been promoted by Mac's insolent behavior.

Watching TV late one evening, I heard a sound outside and discovered that my garage door was open. At that time, Mac had left with a bunch of keys, so I had no way to lock the door I also discovered that windows, which I had left open, had been pushed closed. A while later, I saw shining cell phones through open windows and was woken by noises in the lounge in the early hours of the morning. When I heard sounds coming from the lounge window near my computer, I knew that the Sipho scumbag was after my laptop despite it not being within easy reach. I shouted at him to fuck off and shortly afterwards heard his front door closing. Luckily, I was a night owl and had not yet fallen asleep, but it was obvious that I would have to keep this window closed in the future. Of course, I had to wait for an able-bodied person to come around to help me out or call the Indian neighbor to do so.

These incidents carried on for some time to the point where I was no longer confident that Sipho would not take matters further. One night, I sat with a sharp, serrated butter knife, hoping he would stick his hand through the lounge window near my pc again, relishing in the thought of cutting open his thieving hand. I was disappointed. He probably heard the movement of my wheelchair inside the house and decided to stay out of trouble. Either that or the fact that he knew I was onto him, scared him off. Even if not afraid of me, I was pretty sure he would be afraid of his sister who paid the bills and had the gumption to organize a kangaroo court in the wee hours of the morning.

Because of staying up so late waiting for the scumbag to make a move, I was exhausted after a few hours of sleep and unable to get out of bed to open up for the cleaning lady. This had happened a few times while Mac was still with me. However, with threats and shouting, I was generally able to get him to help me. This particular morning, I ended up calling a friend who had house keys to assist me out of bed. I was in a rage and blamed Mac. I had told him that I would become physically weaker when faced with excessive emotional stress. Obviously, he was in no position to consider this issue given his own health, but I was angry with him anyway. I was also angry with my body for letting me down, knowing that a large portion of my circumstances fell on my shoulders but was unable to contain this internal hot spring of negativity that boiled over when the stresses and challenges of life became excessive.

This threatening situation escalated one morning when I heard the sound of a key in the back door and the back door opening, followed by the sound of someone struggling with the security gate. Tommy jumped off my bed, went down the passage and ran back to my room, releasing a peculiar meow in the process. This was not a sound I had heard from him before, and I knew there was a stranger at the backdoor. Not being able to get out of bed, I called out the name of my cleaning lady. Thankfully, I heard the sound of the back door closing after that, proving to me that someone had gotten hold of the keys. I can only imagine they might have been stolen out of Mac's car or he had flung them onto the grass verge outside the complex when he left. Someone (probably Sipho) could have picked them up, recognized his vehicle or was just taking a chance and trying the keys in every available door in the complex. Whatever the situation, I was grateful when my friend arrived and let herself and my maid in with the spare keys, and they were able to help me get out of bed.

Due to my financial situation, I had been avoiding the necessity of hiring caregivers to help me out of bed in the mornings, with bathing, making food and so on. Still, eventually, I could no longer put this off. Changing the door locks would have to wait. I was glad that my trusty feline companion of the past two years had saved me. I love this cat as if he were my own child, and he will remain with me until one of us passes away. This is my vow to this sentient creature, who has been such an enormous source of comfort and joy to me during my darkest hours on this earth.

As luck would have it, or more pointedly, the universe was taking care of me so well that the one day soon after that, I opened the door to find a young black woman standing on my doorstep looking for work. I told Rose that I couldn't help her but to leave her number with me. She walked off, but that still, small voice inside me told me to call her. She came back. I explained my requirements and how much I could afford to pay. She was happy with the arrangement, although concerned about whether I would be able to cope with her 18-month-old son, whom I later dubbed "Noise Boy." Now, some of my problems were resolved. I had help, but Rose would need time off. Back to Thuli, the 50-year-old lady who had been coming in to clean once a week. An arrangement was made with her and Rose to sleep over three and four days respectively, and everyone was happy. I had help, companionship, and more people in my home, which I also hoped would act as a deterrent to would-be criminals.

Around the middle to end of September 2018, Mac called me three times late one night. I ignored him each time as I was working. On that evening of September 25, I went to bed late as I usually did. From 12 a.m. to 4 a.m., I couldn't sleep. For some reason, I was restless despite having taken my regular dose of cannabis oil. I couldn't understand why I was so agitated. I got up the next morning still feeling really tired, a situation which had become normal. Then I received a phone call. Astrid - girlfriend of Mac's former colleague and long-time friend Lewis - was on the other end of the line. Mac had passed away.

My first response was, "Good." I was happy that he was finally at peace after a miserable, traumatized life coupled with an alcohol addiction that had left him emotionally broken and unable to help himself. However, I felt guilty at my response. Once Astrid's news sank in, I did my crying for his pain, for mine and the grief at what could have been. My response probably seemed very cold to her at the time, but I was past caring what anyone else thought of our relationship. Mac had told his friends so many lies about what was happening that they probably thought that I was a bitch. Actually, I had no energy left to care.

Mac and I had come together to learn lessons, work off Karma or create more. Now, it was over. I held no animosity towards him. He was well loved by so many, including myself, although none of this was going to be enough because Mac hated himself. The tragedy of his life was that he was so talented creatively. And a sensitive, if selfish, bastard. However, his past had caught up with him. He had shuffled off his mortal coil, in Shakespearean terms, after wishing for the one thing he had been so terrified of, and which had been his closest companion for over two decades. Death had come calling, and Mac had answered that call. His loved ones were left to pick up the pieces. Janine organized his funeral in Pretoria from her home in the Eastern Cape. She drove Mac's boys to his funeral. I couldn't go and didn't want to go. Mac had finally been laid to rest. Those who loved him were left to grieve in silence at his passing.

I vacillated between guilt and grief and booked an appointment with a medium in an effort to find out how he was. The medium told me that he was in soul therapy (a new one for me even though I had been an avid reader of all things otherworldly for many years, although I had not spent much time on such matters in recent times). She also told me that any guilt I felt was a consequence of my own insecurities and that Mac needed time away from me to complete his healing process.

Oh, My Word! Yeah! That sounded like the selfish bastard all right, I thought. Ok. *Time to put this puppy to rest,* I told myself, trying to convince myself that my conviction to do so was true. However, I was confused about the sincerity of my reaction to his passing and the unsocially acceptable response, although I had thought that I didn't care too much about what Mac's friends may have thought of how I responded and not attending his funeral. Besides, every time that I thought of Mac, worried about how he was doing, another horrible incident would come to mind where he screwed me over. Small issues would arise, where I found myself swearing at him all over again. The day he packed his goods and left; he spitefully took the cords of my spare pc with him. Every time I opened the front door and it stuck, requiring extra physical exertion on my part to open it, I was reminded of how he had slammed it shut and damaged it, ensuring that I even had difficulty turning the key to lock it. I needed a screwdriver and found that he had emptied my small toolbox. Many such incidents arose after he had left that, for a while, I had trouble moving on. Years later, I would search for my marriage contract to Nelson, only to find that it too, had disappeared. Mac was a spiteful, devious bastard.

I was thankful, however, that he had not passed away while still with me. I don't believe I would have been able to cope with that. Probably, I would have, but I was glad it wasn't necessary. I believe it was the universe looking after me again in its mysterious, intriguing way.

Finally, through all my mixed emotions and thinking how he had stood over me on my one birthday, watching as I struggled to get out of bed and refusing to help me, I felt comfortable with moving on and letting go of my anger towards him.

For years, I had been speaking to my mother once a week to twice a month over the phone. While with Mac, I had longed to speak to her for comfort, but we didn't have that type of relationship. Our communications remained superficial, a duty since I was not particularly fond of her. My anger had been sparked towards my mother once I was old enough to begin making decisions for myself, most of which Mom did not agree with. This had led to resentment as she was emotionally manipulative and controlling. Just like her, I also did not respond well to authority figures. Neither did I react well toward this person who attempted to control every facet of my life. Within approximately a year of completing high school, I had moved out to escape her suffocating ways. Our relationship had not improved over the years. Since moving in with Mac though, I needed her, but we could not be there for one another. I had spoken to her last on Christmas 2017. After that, the opportunity to heal our relationship was all but lost. Mostly, she would simply say "beautiful," which is how she referred to me - one of the few discernible words she uttered after losing her speech.

I spent 2018 speaking to her over WhatsApp whenever one of the nurses at the old age home was prepared to make a phone available. These video calls were brief as Mom was not able to respond, often dropping the phone, leaving me to speak to darkness. During this year of her decline, she experienced several health scares, one of which occurred around March. It prompted Keith to visit from Australia since none of us knew if Mom would pull through. Trevor, Ronald, and Robert also continued making the long trips to visit Mom while my conversations with her continued. We all shared updates on our family WhatsApp group.

A month after Mac passed, we had another health scare regarding Mom. The nurse mentioned that she wasn't sure whether Mom would make it; yet, for some reason, I did not take this seriously. Perhaps because of our physical distance or because Mom had rallied several times over the past year, but I was grateful that several family members were all able to be with her at the end.

On October 26, 2018, I called to speak to Mom while they were with her. Her response was, "Beautiful." She looked poorly but not as if on her deathbed.

I spoke with Ronald, who helped me understand a little better that perhaps her time was approaching. I recorded a message for him to play for Mom, letting her know that she was well-loved and that we supported her decision if she felt it was her time to go. Still, I did not grasp how sick and weak she was. My brothers left her bedside around 7 p.m. after spending the day with her. An hour later, Ronald called me to say that Mom had died. My initial reaction was joy. Although this may seem cold, as with Mac, I was glad that her pain and struggles were over.

My happiness at believing our mother was finally at peace did not last long. Although the physical distance between us had prevented me from being with her at her passing, this distance also provided a buffer between myself and grief. This soon changed as the funeral was arranged, which I was also not able to attend. My brothers shared the service on the WhatsApp group again for those of us who could not be there to honor our mother. This sharing offered some closure. The family arranged to spread half of Mom's ashes along the Port Alfred coastline, which she loved so much, and to save the other half for Keith and myself, for when he was able to return to South Africa. In between, Andi and I had a chat where she offered her support and shared some memories of Mom with me. Between the family members, everyone had different reminiscences to recount as Mom had confided some of her past experiences with one person and not another.

Piecing together portions of her significant events and emotional challenges throughout her life was like a colorful patchwork quilt. Keith shared a poem Mom wrote while visiting him in Australia. It seems particularly poignant as South Africa continues on its own inexorable slide into darkness. I have added the title in the absence of one, since this poem not only captures Mom's secret world of emotion but her thoughts on her spiritual life, which was important to her along with her feelings of the road that our homeland has taken.

No More Fighting

Poem by Mary Murray - January 2003

The call of the bird in the silence
Bring peace, bring peace to our land
No more quarrels, no more fighting
No more raping, pillage, and murder
Only the brotherhood of man.

Stretch out your hand little brother
It is not your desire that you need
But obedience to Christ your Savior
Who gives love and peace to all.

The call of the bird in the silence
Echoes o'er valley and hills
It strikes against ears in the chapel
There the prayers of the faithful ascend.

Stretch out your hand little sister
Accept the love of your Lord
Look to Jesus for all your desires
For His love has conquered the world.

The call of the bird in the silence
Bring love and peace to all.
(Mary Murray 5 August 1932 – 26 October 2018)

This view of Mom's emotions allowed me a greater insight into who she was as a person. In short, I had misunderstood who she was as an individual, a woman, a mother. For so long, I had simply seen her as the person who had raised me - far removed from me emotionally and geographically - who was not nurturing but critical and judgmental, controlling and manipulative. All of these coping strategies had built an insurmountable cocoon around her pain and sadness. As she had become so invisible to others by protecting her inner self, so I began to realize that I had done the same. She had raised me to be strong and independent. In the process, she had also taught me to have massive distrust of others. I had been raised to be a giver, to place myself on the backburner for the pleasure of others. As Mac had lost himself, so had I. I had become my mother - a ball of pain, sadness, rage, anger, and grief for what had been lost. I was not aware of any of this before, with her death being the necessary catalyst to reexamine her as an individual, and myself finally coming into focus.

All of my emotions had been compressed, suppressed, hidden away under a façade of anger and pain simmering like a geyser ready to explode with enough provocation. Now, finally, I understood who Mary Murray was. I was not angry per se – although that had become my forte. My mother was definitely misunderstood, unappreciated as she was unable to demonstrate any vulnerability. When she did, this was misconstrued as overdramatization because of the stark contrast such utterances were to her silent, strong norm - resulting in her feelings being brushed aside as unimportant. Her rejection and abandonment had been learned in her youth and had been carried throughout her life; her coping mechanisms were to hide her pain from others, not wanting to give anyone else the opportunity to see her vulnerabilities or allow them to add any further salt to her already significant emotional wounds.

I realized that, with at least nine miscarriages and six children, Mom had been pregnant for more than 15 years of her adult life. She had given up her first child for adoption; her husband had passed away when she was in her late 30s and still a young woman. She had raised five children on her own after the death of her husband. Mom had endured much pain, which went largely unnoticed and had lived with this pain for close to 80 years. She had experienced so much hurt and had not worked through it. Where Mom had failed in her self-awareness and potential to leave her pain in the past - so had I. We were both walking wounds in a hostile world.

She is now at peace. I realized I had work to do. Internal work. I didn't want to pass this opportunity for inner growth. I faced the greatest challenge of all - to uncover all that hurt, rejection, abandonment fears and to learn to receive, to achieve balance with the final goal of attaining inner peace. The time had come to begin a new journey.

Engaging in this type of internal work seems to be a hit and miss activity. There are no guidelines and few measuring points to say *hey, you've made positive changes*. The alternative though is too terrible to consider - spend the rest of my life with unconscious emotional trauma holding me back or engage in some meditative practices to promote positive change and adjust my perspective on negative memories. I have dabbled with these practices before but did not continue since they are easy in theory, difficult in practice and the outcomes are vague. This time, I intent to persist - between surviving. Few worthwhile changes have ever come without a lot of pain and effort. It is time to take the legacy of my youth and use my knowledge to change the trajectory of my future as so many brave souls had done before me. Will I have the self-discipline and courage to do this? Another time-reliant question that begs for an answer.

Chapter 20

Living with Lyme

I often told myself that I would write a book about my life. My plan had been to write this memoir after I had healed. Since time has taught that this healing is not going to take place until I am prepared to spend time on my inner growth or am the recipient of a miracle of my own healing, I have written it now. Never would I have anticipated the life I have lived while growing up. On learning that a miniscule, infinitely small spirochete/bacteria/germ/bug had so much power to cause misery and destruction was a bitter pill to swallow.

My journey with Lyme began when I was less than a year old and my mother gave me unpasteurized milk. This was followed by a seizure due to a high fever from which I quickly recovered. The bouts of tonsillitis and heavy nosebleeds were put down to childhood ailments rather than anything more sinister. Full body rashes and fevers followed as I acquired two new tick infections on separate occasions, accompanied by a brief bout of anemia, which was quickly sorted out with a supplement. Much, much worse was to follow as my muscles began to mysteriously weaken as a teenager. Fear of the unknown set in as all those doctors in their white coats, many with the arrogant attitudes to accompany their long years of learning, failed to provide an accurate diagnosis. My world felt as if it was caving in on itself as I set out on a road to self-destruction with alcohol and men.

Later, I had no choice but to take the step of using a manual wheelchair and then a motorized wheelchair. My confusion was so overwhelming that there was no thought of blaming God or anyone else; rather I experienced frustration at the lack of answers. It just wasn't feasible that I had developed a disease that was untreatable and incurable. Some 30 years later, filled with a sense of acceptance, inevitability, and resignation, I learned that this disease would have, could have, been quite easily curable; that I would in all likelihood have recovered without further health issues.

Even during the brain fog, I had managed to acquire my degree in business management, swimming through a thicket of information to retain enough to achieve decent grades. You may not understand the concept of brain fog as it is not immediately obvious and may never be. However, it robs victims of clear thought, making the simplest processes a challenge at times. Add to this the stresses of everyday life, and I found myself further frustrated at not being able to express myself succinctly or forgetting words that had previously come easily to mind. Adding insult to injury, this disease also caused hair loss. Where the hairdresser had earlier needed two lots of a product to perm my hair, now one batch was too much. Balding as a woman and in my 40s was an insult. Unfortunately, it was just one more offense that this disease was capable of, among so many others. Lyme disease has robbed me of my health and had almost completely wrecked my entire life with the collateral damage caused to my personality, mood swings and emotional turmoil that I brought with me to every relationship I impulsively pursued - not comprehending the heartache I was setting myself up for at the time.

For me, a typical day begins with one of my rotating caregivers helping me out of bed. Up until about six months ago (mid-2018), I was still able to get myself out of bed albeit with some difficulty. I would wake up from lying on my right side all night since I am too weak to turn over. I would lick the back of my left hand, place this at the back of my right leg just at the bend of my knee to draw my bottom leg closer to my chest, having enough movement in my left leg while lying down to draw this closer to my chest. In a fetal position, I would then use my neck as a fifth limb and "walk" myself into position with my head facing away from my wheelchair parked alongside my bed. When in this position, I would then attempt to move my buttocks onto my feet and then inch backwards until I could get my rear end into the wheelchair seat, and my feet slipped off the side of the bed. Then, I would push myself into an upright position from there.

This ability faded away. Now, to get out of bed, I need caregivers to maneuver me so that I can sit in a folded position on my feet before I can perform this activity - a frustrating situation to say the least.

Getting into bed is also a tiring, time-consuming, cumbersome process. To succeed, I drive my wheelchair to the edge of my bed, clasp my interlaced fingers around my right knee, lift my leg using momentum rather than strength to swing the front portion of my foot onto my bed. This maneuver is followed by reversing, so that I can swing the right foot rest out to the side of my wheelchair; repeat with the left side, bum walk to the middle of my bed until my feet are hanging over the other side; fall to my right, draw my knees to my chest with some hand licking for traction - otherwise I cannot gain enough grip to move my legs - do the neck/head walk, pulling my legs after me until I can rest my head on my pillow. Then, I need to take my left leg, get my knee into position behind my right calf to straighten my right leg as much as possible, using my hand to push on my right thigh to help this process along until I am finally comfortable enough to close my eyes and rest in reasonable comfort.

I use a toilet seat raiser, which is simply a gadget placed on a normal toilet to raise it to the level of my wheelchair seat as I don't have enough strength in my arms to lift my body weight. Going to the toilet then is simply a matter of pushing my pants down far enough so that once I have slid onto the toilet seat, it is easier to remove them further. This is one reason I never go out anymore as it is impossible to carry a toilet seat raiser all over with me, even assuming that my wheelchair can fit into any normal bathroom, which it seldom can. Even if there is enough room for a wheelchair, public toilets are mostly made to accommodate children and other little people or simply to save contracting costs when building, so the seats are too low for me to navigate. I'm not sure why this is the case, but I have seen hospitals where the toilets were so low to the ground that it was difficult to imagine any sick person being able to use these without assistance. Then again, another hospital had "disabled" bars, meant to be installed alongside the toilet and on the wall directly behind it - several meters up, with personnel using these bars to hang items on. This level of ignorance, stupidity or just plain negligence and incompetence no longer upsets me. I live in a world where this is expected and commonplace, where wheelchair parts are so expensive and appear to be designed by stupid engineers or set up to break within a couple of weeks of purchase, such as the almost paper-thin plastic bases that are screwed into the armrests. When I place a little weight on the armrests, the plastic base quickly cracks, allowing those sharp screws to eventually pop through their thin overlay of sponge - just to add to what is already a very challenging day, to be repeated over and over again. A bit like the movie *Groundhog Day*.

At least I sleep better now. Eight years on antibiotics has helped to cleanse my liver enough to allow for improved rest. My headaches disappeared after a few months on antibiotics, also enhancing my life quality to some degree. Any lack of sleep is now overcome with cannabis oil, although stress overrides even this at times. Also, I cannot take enough cannabis oil to deal with the insidious pain that I can barely feel, but I know is there when I become inordinately tired. Then, it is time to pop a Mypaid tablet. The combination of the Ibuprofen anti-inflammatory and the Paracetamol painkiller are enough to stave off the exhaustion and pain and help me feel better within a couple of hours.

Bathing or showering myself is no longer possible. That's why I now have two caregivers to assist me throughout the day. I can barely open the fridge or make a sandwich anymore. Still being able to type seems to be a miracle, and I cannot help but wonder what my life will be like if I lose the strength in my neck or the ability to type anymore. What then? A beached whale? A talking head? A female Stephen Hawking without the brain or the finances? As bleak as the future may seem, I am not without hope that I will be able to dig below the iron-clad wall of exhaustion, that there is something better and that it will be of my own design. Depression after the loss of Mom and Mac - in conjunction with a physical disease whose progress has moved from inexorably slow to speeding up as I have matured - might be a terrifying prospect for many. Experience and time have taught me though that this journey is indeed one of a thousand and more steps. Depression is an additional challenge to be surmounted every day, made even more challenging by the stresses of making ends meet.

These thoughts flow through my mind as I drift back, recalling how I told Mom to have more faith many years ago, realizing now that this sage advice was applicable to myself in the present. Although raised in the Anglican church, I had long since drifted away from the manipulations of this manmade source of control. Instead, my interests had taken me down a far more esoteric path, one where energy and the quantum mysteries of life still await to be unraveled by intrepid individuals, preferably devoid of politics. My fascination for the world of the unseen remains almost as strong although the pressing responsibility of survival had largely supplanted this thirst for knowledge in recent times.

I still believe that emulating models like Jesus and Buddha is the way to go for peace and other positive change. I had, in fact, taken a leaf out of the Christian Science book, which attempts to explain the Christian Bible, the most misinterpreted, misconstrued collection of writings of all time, to practice self-healing. Using the "I am light, I am life, I am love, I am truth, I am spirit, I am soul, I am that I am" affirmation from *Science and Health with Key to the Scriptures* had increased my strength many years earlier. Due to doubt and a lack of self-confidence, I saw the results, perceived them with disbelief and stopped practicing, allowing my memory to revert to an uneasy status quo.

As I struggle to raise a cup of coffee to my mouth, using two hands to accomplish this task, learning to ignore an itch on my back because my fingers don't have the strength to scratch it and so many other challenges that characterize my daily life, I wonder again whether there are others who can take some inspiration from my world. Will the fact that I refuse to give up spur them on to accomplish their dreams? Will the fact that I was taught so much resilience and persistence by my mother motivate them to pick up the pieces of their own broken lives to face a new day, with renewed hope and strength in the knowledge that this is simply an opportunity to learn, grow, become better, to become the best they can be as I am attempting to do. At the end of the day, we all must face our own struggles and meet these with the resources we have, however limited they may be.

In some ways, then, I am still back in the idyllic days spent decades ago in Keiskammahoek, ever optimistic and looking towards a better future.